Morph in a Minute

Magic in the Moment = Ravings of a Medium

Susan Bellwether

authorHOUSE®

AuthorHouse™
1663 Liberty Drive
Bloomington, IN 47403
www.authorhouse.com
Phone: 1-800-839-8640

First published by AuthorHouse   3/24/2010

ISBN: 978-1-4490-9617-5 (e)
ISBN: 978-1-4490-9616-8 (sc)

Library of Congress Control Number: 2010903190

Printed in the United States of America
Bloomington, Indiana

This book is printed on acid-free paper.

Morph in a Minute
Magic in the Moment
=Ravings of a Medium

By Sue Bellwether
M.A. from Columbia University
Reiki Master

Dedication

I dedicate this book to my four children, to my siblings, to my parents, and to Adam who died.

Acknowledgements

Special thanks to Ymane for finally kicking me in the butt to get this book written. Thank you to Sarah and Kaitlin for holding me up. Thank you to Maggie for propelling me to change. Thank you to Paige for helping me type.

Please note that all names have been changed to protect identities of any persons mentioned in the following material.

Preface

Life can be full of challenges. Hopefully there will be change when you want it. May you find strength in the messages from beyond imparted to you here. Dead people morph quickly. May you morph in a minute as quickly as they do.

I use the word morph as an abbreviated form of metamorphosis .This can be interpreted as change and transformation in one's internal state of thinking , feeling or being and the manifestation thereof.

Contents

WHO AM I

WHEN I LOOK AT ME, I CAN SOMETIMES SEE RIGHT THROUGH MY EYES TO THE OTHER SIDE. AND WHEN I LOOK INTO YOUR EYES, I CAN SEE RIGHT THROUGH YOU.

I am a human with a soul encased in my body and my story is as worthy of being told as anyone else's. My story is as interestingly valid as yours and yours is as interestingly valid as mine merely because we are humans on this earth unfolding the path of our soul's evolvement. My path is unique and beautiful and it belongs to no one else. That makes our life special.

I believe that I bring love to love. It is my job as a light worker to bring people's understanding to a place where it is perceived that we are not alone. Even though this life is tough, we have love in the guides above us. Our universe works in interesting and unseen ways. The incarnation of the soul into human bodies is its chosen path to perfection. Lessons comprise all of our existence. The soul basically takes on the appearance of the physical body in its effort to relate to other souls on this planet as it endeavors to overcome its imperfections and trials.

The dictionary defines psychic as "of the soul" and "apparently sensitive to the forces beyond the physical world." The definition of medium is " an intervening thing through which a force acts or an effect is produced" and "a middle state" as well as "any means agency or instrumentality" and "a person through whom communications are supposedly sent from the dead to the living." I have those aspects of my being. What I do is a labor of love which is defined as "work that one enjoys doing - any work done or task performed with eager willingness either from fondness for the work or from the regard one has for the person or the cause for whom it is done."[1]

The information I get comes from the beings that watch over us- all deceased relatives ,spirit guides, angels and of course Spirit. I receive information from live souls as well; for when I open my window they come with messages too. So, when I say "They said" that is the set of informants and guardians of information to which I am referring. What makes a reading a reading is not imagination, wishing or guessing. It is kind of like I go up, they come down and we meet at the half way point. This offers hope that there is another dimension. You do not necessarily see it but it is there. It has the potential to take your pain away for even a second. I am a medium. I am like the artist's charcoal or paint. I am something intermediate. I feel like I raise my vibration to meet them halfway. They lower theirs to meet mine.

In a reading, there should be a dance. It is not a test of anything but bringing the person being read love. Connecting him to the other side is what occurs and the bottom line is that he feels better. The souls on the other side are ecstatic to be able to finally contact their loved ones when somebody like me raises my vibration and escalates to the level of speed at which they exist. It should not be a test of my ability, it should be the conscious effort of both the person being read and myself that she become cognizant of the other side. Potentially she will

---

[1] Webster's New Universal Unabridged Dictionary. Copyright 1983.

feel a little relief, hope and faith and ultimately love. It is fun if I say a name and he recognizes his brother or I say that Aunt Alice is here with her famous blueberry pie. It is amazing if a spirit comes through and apologizes for having been neglectful. There is another dimension. It is not just about what you are going through now. There is a whole other part of or transition of the human that exists and with which we can communicate. Hope should follow a reading and love is always part of it.

When I look at me I can sometimes see right through me to the other side. When I look into your eyes I can see right through you.

I believe that we incarnate in these bodies from the soul world. It is kind of like the soul puts on a coat of human cover, and it comes off when you die. Death is like ice cubes changing to water. Pieces of energy of which we are all composed are always moving. We are made of a bunch of particles which are in motion and therefore we are in motion in a physical and spiritual sense. The dead beings function at a higher vibration. The human vibration is lower. To reiterate I can travel to the higher vibration by raising mine and they come down and we meet in the middle or their half speed. I interchange the word soul and spirit when I talk in my readings. The spirit is who is talking to me. It is the manifestation of the personality of the soul which has passed back into spirit world. I know that there is no way I could receive the information I do in any other way. It happens on a daily basis. The other vibration informs me of things. These are verified by those whom I am reading.

I was somewhere in the quiet place I call it (others would say the soul place or higher vibration) I guess until sometime in 1950 when I decided with my guides

3

undoubtedly to come down here with the brilliant plan of becoming Sue Bellwether.

I was one of four children. Everyone should realize that each child in a family has the same two parents but also completely different parents. Just because I am a psychic does not mean my life is all peaches and cream. I would say it is peaches and cream with the pit. My mother does not remember what time I was born on that day exactly, but she remembers what time my brother was born and that was 10:32. That tells you something about where I stood in the family. The first born son could do no wrong. I was the second child, a daughter, and as such was raised differently. My little baby sister was the spoiled one. At the time she was born, both my father and other sister were dethroned, allied and she became his favorite by a mile. But of course my parents were a product of their generation, the mass consciousness at the time, their karma and their contracts that their souls had made. Each child has his own soul lessons and individual contracts with each member of the family. On a secular and spiritual level too, even though they were parents of four children, they were different parents for all of the above reasons for each of the four children.

But that having been said, I had a great upbringing. I am happy I was raised the way I was. I am happy about who I have become and who I am continuing to become. We had a pretty peaceful upbringing with mild challenges and basically high aspirations for all of us . We were well fed and clothed, educated and of course loved. Apart from mild discrepancies, our family was solid with my parents' marriage lasting 50 years with them being very functional and in love, providing a good role model. They were good citizens and solid parents.

The rest of my story begins with a memory I have of being six months old. I was belly down on a striped towel at my beach house and upon a simple request to have their picture taken with me, my two grandfathers squabbled over who was going to hold me. They tossed me back and forth somewhat like a football and my mother finally took one picture of each grandfather holding me.

The next memory jumps to me being about two and we were on a boat going to Martha's Vineyard. I remember looking at all the kids drinking orange soda from a glass bottle. I asked my parents for one and they said "No, you will spill it. I said "No I won't." My mother discussed it briefly with my father and they finally consented. She opened the metal lid and handed the bottle to me .My father sat with legs crossed looking at me skeptically thinking he would watch as I spilled it all out. I drank every bit of that orange soda without spilling a drop.

I jump ahead to being about three - a very significant year for me. My grandfather had me on his knee and offered me some time tickling his mustache. He died within weeks after that. I jump to a few months later. I was very happy with my imaginary friend. Her name was "Jackie". I told my mother all about it and had my mother set a place for her at the dinner table. My mother took me to the Doctor. She had no idea what else to do. The Doctor said I needed friends. I was fine. There were no nursery schools in those days who took children in at that early age. However summer was soon coming and I heard talk that my five year old brother was going to camp. I asked my mother if I could go. "You are too young" she said. I persisted and so she called the camp director. I remember her standing there arguing with him telling him I really wanted to go even though I was three. He finally asked " Can she tie her shoes?" She said "No". He said "Well if she could then we would try her out". I said when my mother got off the phone that I wanted her to immediately teach me how. She said to my father "What should I do? Should I teach her?" He said " Sure, what the heck, she will never get it." My mother went back to the stove to cook her dinner. I remember she was wearing her white cotton shirt and had her pixie hair cut. She turned around and bent down to me and taught me how to make a loop and twist the lace around but I did not get it. Then she brightened and said, " Wait a minute. I remember now how my father taught me to tie my shoes. You make two bunny ears, cross them and you bring one around." Well you know the rest. I learned how to tie my shoes! I practiced all night. Then I went to bed. In the morning I gave it a try first thing. I completely forgot. But after a quick refresher course, I finally could tie my shoes perfectly . My mother called the camp director and I enrolled with his "give it a try" attitude even though I was so very young. I stayed in camp all summer, and my imaginary friend never returned. I now recognize she must have been a spirit. Now I see lots of spirits, but on very special occasions. I will see them in my readings.

When I was seven, every night I would see colors as I lay trying to fall asleep. I asked my mother what the colors were. She said " There are no colors. It is dark, just go to sleep." I saw the colors. I tested whether I saw them with my eyes open or shut. They were always in front of me. They looked like paisley flakes of color. I never mentioned it again to anyone. Every night , the colors which seemed friendly to my way of thinking, and I went to sleep. I am told that spirits may appear like specks of light as well and that is basically to what I attribute my color perception. I never thought of surreal things again until my early forties.

At four I used to walk back and forth to school by myself much to my mother's chagrin and my insistence. In those days it was much safer. I was very independent, but very shy in the classroom. As time passed I was always with the same kids in that neighborhood and progressed through high school with basically the same kids in all the gifted classes. I was clearly with bright kids and rich kids and accelerated kids in their physical and social development. I was the tiniest one and the slimmest and less curvy of the buxom girls. The experience I can see now helped me remain humble and quiet as well as reserved. There were very mouthy over confidant boys too. The humility my parents manifested even though they were educated and accomplished, as well as the humility I had growing up with this noisy socially rambunctious cocky group of bright kids who never changed, kept me at a place where humility and yet quiet confidence set me apart. I developed an ability to know who I was and yet feel a bit overshadowed. Humility I think is a great part of why spirits let me do this. I am honoring at all times what they let me do and have no arrogance about it. My ego is superseded by intuition and soul awareness. If human perception reigned, I believe that would taint any accuracy in the readings and inhibit spirits from choosing one. I am chosen to be the conduit of love because I am pure. I have gone through a lot of my own sifting through issues and some trauma, neglect, abuse and facing the above as a learning human covering the soul; but I remain faithful to the insight that I can bring love to people. I have the feeling that the other dimension floats through more freely if the being they are using as the medium is more pure and light and caring and humble. Arrogance is a vice and not pure. It blocks what would otherwise be a wide channel. I am a light worker proving that there is more than meets the eye and even more that meets the heart. For the heart is two fold- ego and soul elements exist within it.

I grew up got married and divorced after twenty-one years of a lousy marriage but that is another book. I bore four children who are the light of my life, and their lives at the moment shall remain theirs and totally off limits until they want to be known publicly. With hindsight I see the main reason for that marriage, was to bring forth into the world those four children. My job was to raise them to be authentically themselves. At the end of our marriage was when I met Adam at the store which was owned by my ex. My ex had a female compadre and I had Adam and it was in no way covert. We double dated and were all real good friends- we knew the marriage was disintegrated and we were trying to be civil and live together for the kid's sake, but of course that ended later on. Adam was my phenomenally close soul mate. He was clearly the most intense, short relationship I have ever experienced. I knew him for only a year and then he was dead.

We had become really fast friends. He had come into the retail store that my husband and I owned. I felt a connection with him immediately. He came in and asked if we carried garlic salt and said that he cooked with it a lot. He came in the next week with his son and bought some more. He was smart and knew that if he charged it, they would call me up for the charge. So he did, and I went up and we talked more. He was 39. I liked his mind and perceptions. We were lovers for seven months, do not worry, my ex had someone too. When you make a soul connection there is an amazing feeling of familiarity of friendship built in days or weeks that would have otherwise taken years even if it had arrived at that point.

I fell for him the day that we took a row and I was telling him about my neglect- filled marriage. I, who rarely cry, felt a tear running down my left eye. When I looked at him he had a tear for me rolling out of his right eye. Shortly after I thought he was going to be my next mate, he took a trip to Portugal to become more familiar with techniques to teach the language, where he at the age of 40 suddenly died. He had a two week ticket. Before he left I had my first as far as I can remember, psychic thought. I said to myself as I was meeting him for what would turn out to be the last time I ever saw him, "What if I never see you again?" We both thought that was ridiculous since he had just turned from thirty nine years old to forty and since he had a two week ticket. Well that catapulted me beyond the periphery of Susan and into a whole other existence. During that week I was able to receive one phone call from him. He was as I said, in Portugal across the ocean. I had gone to the beach to reflect on the news that people had heard he got sick over there, and I saw my first psychic board form in front to the right of me. The words floated on like a cork board. They said myocardial infarction. I had no idea what was happening but he called. I asked him what they said he had, and he said "myocardial infarction." He died several days later. I was a basket case. I never thought I would get out of that low place. He died but that was the beginning of my psychic life. When he died, I felt like I was unzipped and my insides were outside. That is the closest set of words I can find. It took two months for me to hear this strange noise coming from myself and I finally realized it was laughter. During this time I was approached by Reiki people who were related to a friend of mine and I took the courses hoping for anything to make me feel better. They were the only people I had ever met who believed in the afterlife.

A year of learning more about Reiki and energy kept me hoping somewhat that the truth was that there is more than this. Reiki can be somewhat shortened in definition as channeling the life force or universal force for healing emotionally as well as physically.

Concurrently I had this lump growing on my thyroid. I had had half of it removed when I was twenty four, and the thing was growing back. I had no other symptoms and felt great. In an attempt to avoid surgery I went to the world of spiritual healers of which I had become aware. I went to several each of whom had her own modality. I had no idea what one did, but she would touch me gently on the forehead and I would be gone out of my body somehow - seeing visions and hoping this would do the trick. I am pretty sure the idea was that the soul has a perfect blueprint, so the body stays on that table, while the soul goes up to try to reprogram itself to then come back down to the body with a better if not perfect blueprint and correct the ailment of that body. Also I tried acupuncture hoping for similar results but that did not work to eliminate the lump either. I finally tried this other individual on a friend's recommendation. Something interesting happened there. She led me through a relaxed state into whatever vision I might arrive at and in not even hypnotherapy or trance I suddenly recognized myself in a prison in the 1600's. I did not look exactly the same but there was a knowing that it was I. I was imprisoned because I was an herbal expert of come kind and some parents had brought me a sick baby to try to heal and I did what I could but the baby still died. I was imprisoned as a witch. The message in the vision of the soul's past life I would call it was that this is not that time. And the gifts that I have can be used now and I will not be imprisoned. All of the modalities I have been describing I believe raised my vibration and helped get me here. In addition being not very attached to material things as well as taking the plunge to work through my issues unlayering them like an onion- contributes to my abilities, too. I consented in the end to get the surgery and am now a firm believer in east and west medicine being a marriage. I did have unbeknownst to me at the time a six inch piece of cancer in my neck. I believe I charted that illness as well as the healers I met on my journey precisely to become who I have become. I sure was stubborn throughout adhering to what I felt was the path, much to the chagrin of every relative who shared my last name, my maiden name and pretty much anyone who noticed that physical deformity that once rested on my thyroid. Soon psychic occurrences began to happen.

Those are the surprising comments I have about how I became a psychic and medium. I continue to evolve. At first my psychic board showed the words as a

I said. Then I started to see black and white 16mm type movies. Then they changed to living color. It was always kind of like looking into a pond the way the reflection looks. The spirits, who I demand only come if they are in the light, always say loving important things and things particular to the individual I am reading. I did the first thousand readings for free, and then child support went down and I started charging. I am very cheap actually. I exchanged things like a can of tuna fish or a hug earlier. Now it is a valued commodity. I one day realized that if some one could buy an orange today at a store, they could buy me telling them that the spirits love them , are okay and tell them something as specific as "you forgot to buy new curtains for your house".

As I go through my life now I am more and more aware of the way I can communicate with the other world, or that they have chosen me to do it. It is a rewarding feeling when tears that have waited to fall for decades land in my hands. Spirits offer apologies, accolades of praise for a relative, and knowledge of grandchildren born long after they transitioned to the other side. This affirmation of accurate facts always amazes me as well as the people I am reading.

I am just a person on the outside, very skinny. I eat junk food, walk a few hours a day, enjoy the sky and the ocean and horses and a lot of ice cream and visiting my mother and adoring my children whether they are in my thoughts or I am lucky enough to have them in my house. All the while I know the spirits are about to relay some amazing piece of affirmation to me, any minute now. It is an amazing expectant feeling. It happens often and sometimes I feel like I spend more time over there. It is peaceful there, it is quiet usually . It feels lighter and colors are different and pretty much all the communication is without moving any mouths. There is a knowing that instantaneously happens. I know what they are communicating. I know exactly what they are saying about the personalities of the descendents or loved ones. All of my readings have had amazing insight, affirmations by the spirits naming names for the people of their deceased relatives who speak of their own characteristics. They come through with apologies, little anecdotal comments, statements that they watched the person that very day, and any good reading also will have tools which the person that is being read can use to better their lives. This proves that this is not all there is by a long shot.

Sometimes I am talking to someone and the spirit will show me their house- like where the couch is and that there is a dog with a blue bow sitting on it when he is not supposed to be. I have been shown houses in other countries affirmed by the architecture and landscape I describe. Details can be interesting and very moving. The stories are the truth of the readings. Whether you believe in the after life or not, whether you believe that I am real, in that the spirits help me intuit or communicate other worldly things to me does not matter. What does matter, is that you feel better when you think there is hope that there might be a world beyond. It is hard to go through life thinking "This is it ? This is all there is?This is all the stuff I have gone through, what could it possibly be for?" Bringing the thought and the hope of possibility is crucial. So love and expecting to hear from the dead is what makes me tick right now. I hope all of you can come to me or access an informative reading and you will be amazed, happy or relieved and morph in a minute.

PHILOSOPHY

THE SPIRITS HAVE IMPARTED THESE WORDS OF WISDOM TO ME. TRY TO FOLLOW THEM AND YOU MAY MORPH.

We must be made aware if we are to be happy in this life that this is an illusion. We are merely the coat that the soul is wearing. Inside us resides a powerful piece of spirit. The illusion is that we are confined by what we think a human can only do. Truth be told the innate creations of the soul can be manifested in the reality of the participating human. This is true because the possibility of anything exists in the blueprint of the soul. There can be magic in the world. In other words, the illusion that the human is all there is is dispelled. We now know that it merely houses like a vehicle, the soul that is actually supposed to drive. The thought that we are now souls in human bodies thus presents the case that the world must be perceived differently. The illusion that humans are all that is means that one looks at the world with a finite limiting false reality. Now we see that the souls create limitless possibility and magic becomes available to our paradigm. The paradigm shifts from density of the man or woman or child to freedom to grow ,evolve and imagine limitless magical moments from here to infinity. This sense and knowing that magic can happen is key to changing our behavior. When you realize that life on this planet is entirely an illusion-that being that it is not populated by humans, it is populated by humans encasing incarnated souls, then magic can happen in the moments produced by the souls in the bodies of the humans.

They said when I went to the beach one day that the tide comes in and out. Things come and go. Good times weave up and down and forward and back. The rhythm of the ocean is like that rhythm in life. In the seeming free reign good times come in when we do not expect them. They leave and periods of growth come in as the good times leave. The bad, fretful evil times also come as the tide goes out but in those times we realize that there is no stopping and starting and the bad times will leave, too.

It sometimes seems like we cannot do anything more about the rhythm of good and bad times then we can do about our heartbeat. It goes on and we go on around it but supplied and supported and alive because of it. Likewise, our rhythm of good and bad supports us, and we are going on along with it and because of it we are evolving.

It is hard to tell where I stop and the universe starts. When you ask for something you are really looking inside yourself for tools to be put in motion. In a sense the universe and you are one, the tools of the universe are your tools. You are made of the same materials as the stars and the sky. You are about 60% water- the same as the sea. You have the power to change. You hold the same power to have what you want, to be what you want, as the universe has to change, be, or do what it wants. The reason for this is because we are all part of the same scene. We are on earth. This is our illusion together. Look into the eyes of the person beside you. You are his left arm and he is your right. We are all souls made of the same stuff. We are all on this same spaceship Earth together.

We incarnate in specific groups and I believe in reincarnation as well. The various souls take on different personalities in various lifetimes but continue to be together throughout time and lessons. The ultimate test is how much you have given unconditional love to others. There is a test of endurance in the incarnations on both the physical as well as the soul level. The efforts required to endure the hardships of this plane of existence are intensely difficult at times. The endurance of the love in the spiritual world is an inescapable fact. The truth is that it is always there while we are continually challenged down here. So, yes, endurance comes in the form of stretching beyond your limits; while at the same time feeling the limitless endurance of the love even on the other side of all the people you have ever known in life. Again, it is a continuum of intense unrelenting love from the other side pouring down on you concurrently. I am blessed to make people aware of this two way street.

The universe has a plan to end things the way they are supposed to end. The universe is working. Let it work. I am not suggesting that you sit in your room with the door shut. Get out and find yourself in the flow of things. Remember anything can happen. You may not now or never know why things are happening now; but remember the fluidity. Nothing lasts forever. The good does not last forever. The bad does not last forever. This feeling you have right now does not last forever. Happy elation does not last. One minute you hit a grand slam in the baseball game and the next time you strike out. That is the flow you are in and you keep playing. You will hit the fence. There is no stopping and starting in the ever changing game of baseball or life. I, many times in my life, even wonder about the calendar. Man made it. In a way, who needs it? Why can't life be viewed more like I view it in that it can be one long period ?

A lot of people do believe that you bring your gifts from your prior lives to your present life and you may use them or not. I do not believe it is a vertical line. I think there are different lessons. You may come in to work on one issue while another one takes a back seat. Certain talents you have may not manifest in this lifetime but they remain as gifts in your soul to reappear some other time. There is a dimension of souls who have struggled so hard previously and appear to have earned a happy life this time. There are many issues, underpinnings, and charts in these lives but it all balances. Understand that no matter what you are going through, it will be resolved.

I believe that we incarnate in these bodies from the soul world. We house these souls and it is like you snap yourself up into a Susan suit or button yourself into a Jay suit or whatever your name is. You unsnap and unbutton it when you die. I think that souls incarnate in groups. They come together and have agreements with each other that they will work on their issues in the form of persons they become, as I have said. You have levels of soul mates. Your soul mates extend out into concentric circles and include your children, parents, closest friends, mates, workmates, etc. Sometimes you even linger looking at somebody and you find yourself looking too long and they, you. One time I was walking up the street and I was feeling particularly sad after the breakup of the one woman with whom I eventually had a relationship, and a neighbor that had just moved from Florida that I did not know that well, poked her head out the door .She peeked out and gave me the biggest grin and said, "Good morning! How are you?" It was the first and nearly last conversation I had with her, but it made such a difference that day. Even little moments can remind you that you are a soul. It does not mean that you will have a phenomenal relationship with everyone you meet. However, sometimes the souls in people's bodies look out and you see the light shining and you say, "Oh yes," this is not just a material world and there are souls inside. The little things you do make a difference.

Your soul sets up the arrangements you have with your intimate soul mates. Wherever you work and the different things you do, different experiences you have during the day are props for you do learn unconditional love and learn your lessons.

I think we incarnate- souls come into human bodies- and try to learn lessons, the most pressing of which is unconditional love. There are other challenges like separation, addiction, self-concept issues which are all fertile ground for embracing some soul growth. To the best of my knowledge souls incarnate in groups by prior arrangement made in the quiet place. There are agreements to come in and work through their lessons together. In the form of the persons they become, the souls bounce off each other by mirroring issues or pushing the other person to the wall of change . Potentially the adversity of so many situations and experiences morphs the people involved. The potential is there and the possibility for evolving the quickest way from point A to point B is the best route to take. I think there is a plan B if someone has fallen away from their original path's blueprint. Another individual may come along to help implement the original premise. The players may change but the lesson is the same. A person can fall off chart much like a ball rolling down the bowling alley. Bumper guards are put in place for wayward fellows. Once again the opportunity to get pushed back on track is offered. Some souls will in their bodies accomplish Plan A and some will not partake of the opportunities for their soul to evolve; I think after enough opportunities are dismissed some souls will remain on the low end of the continuum. Some will excel and get an A plus, continuing to grow here and thus arriving at a super place in the next world on the other side.

There are lessons to be learned every step of the way. Nothing is random. I do not think the color shirt you wore today is that significant, but being at certain places at particular times, or who your best friends are, or how functional your relationships with your grandparents are, or who your football teammates are, or who your priest is, or who your neighbors are, or who you meet at the ice cream place, is random at all. I think you are given opportunities in these experiences to have the quickest path to the highest soul movement on the continuum of evolvement. If you take it- great. then your stay in what I may repeat from the spirits in 'the motel of mirrors" on this planet can shorten your trip to the "joint of joy"- not in time, but in acceleration on reaching your highest point of evolvement. The mirror concept is that you hook up with people who have your same issues and they mirror you and even make you look at yourself in an exacerbated way by being even moreso. We are attracting someone who is at the same place we are on the continuum.

All of the experiences and people with whom we interact are props to learn our lessons. We are to experience and chart things to overcome in order to perfect our souls. You can look and say I do not want to be like that. You may say this self esteem or addiction or abuse or abandonment issue is so awful that I do not want to be like that .The mirrors manifest your behaviors to seem so large in your eyes that you see yourself in their pattern of existence and then you can overcome it.

An addict will very often attract an addict. The particular issue may be different. One may be addicted to alcohol; another to cigarettes or food. The issue however is the same. One mate may be angry about his mother and the other angry about her child abuse. What is key is that both people are angry and they have attracted each other to see anger and hopefully work through it. The opportunity is there for you to grow up, face the music and roll on. If you both grow, and there is harmonious evolution occurring at the same time, you can still stay together and closely hold your human relationship as you both travel.

You are creating your story as you go along. It is not the story of the person two houses away from you on your street; or your sister's story or your child's story. There are so many factors in what happens like karma, your specific chart and also the contracts you made in terms of what you choose to accomplish while here. I believe when you are born the day you are going to die is also known and can vary with probably a 6 month window on either side. People need to learn to morph quickly, as the dead have it way more in control. People obsess about their dramatic stresses on a minute to minute basis and drag arguments out and various postures and sides, needs and personal desires to the hilt. Dead people morph in about a second from one state to another.

Challenges become fertile ground for embarking on soul growth. One may need to learn patience, or attachments, or independence or self esteem. When you finally learn all your lessons through all your incarnations you can go back and live with God in that world or come back down as a mother Theresa, or such. The main lesson to be learned is unconditional love, what you take with you is how well you did that. Forgiveness is pivotal as well; what I have learned is you can not judge anybody. When you forgive somebody their path, because you do not know what is right for them, you feel better.

You do the very best you can in any situation and do not be attached to the outcome. One never knows what happens next. Why this or that path unfolds and this contact is made or that connection arises is something that is seen well with hindsight but not very often before a metamorphosis occurs do you see the relatively straight line leading up to it.

Life is a hard thing to progress through. It is easy to get stuck. Anger is a huge block. Anger and love can not exist in the same place. It is key to be mad; then realize you are only going to bury yourself deeper in the quicksand if you live there. The beauty of the world will pass you by. When you blame everything else for your circumstances then you begin to take away your own power . To get unstuck you need to stop blaming everyone else for your feeling victimized and start taking chances and your power will come back little by little. You will morph when you realize that you had the power all along to get out of the situation that debilitates you and your forward progression can begin. You kind of lose soul points if you stay too long in a situation that pulls your soul backwards into a cycle of repeated abuse.

Remember that this is our planet. We have to make the best of it. We are always moving. Do not worry if you seem stuck. You have the opportunity to move. You are always being presented with challenges that I am constantly reminded are growing times by the spirits. It is always up to you whether you take full advantage of them. I sure like the quickest road from one place to another.

If you are ever sad know that you are always moving; picture a water faucet. The water is streaming as a unit, the way you see it. Slow it down and then you will see little droplets that are separate .They look like they are dense, that is what people are. We are little pieces of energy always moving and gyrating and dancing. The enlightened beings are feeling lighter all the time. The people who have not yet awakened tend to feel dense and tired. They are grouchy, mad and starved for love and affection. They are without the wonder and joy in the universe. Dead people are merely changed in this energy state. I repeat it is sort of like ice cubes changing to water. (For me they appear almost like when you look into a pool and see a reflection.)

The water never stays still and neither do you. If you have ever watched a baby transform, you see the movement or propulsion from stage to stage. If you are sad you are on the way to being happy. If you are happy you will be challenged soon and the intensity of a situation will make you or offer you a growing period. We are all in movement, changing ourselves and our souls, our personality in the path of becoming. Just becoming-becoming once again when we can still cross over the veil-when it will be invisible and everyone will live in a world of no judgment - no fat no thin no black no white-when we are all equal and light and peaceful-bright and in God's land.

But we are not all perfect, but in a way, we are. We all have a piece of perfection in us because we all have a speck of God in us. Our soul has a blueprint that originated over there and therefore we match our personalities to our souls. We can be perfect, but we are all struggling to do that. We are in a way capable of doing what we want to do, having what we want to have, being what we want to be. I think some people do not tap into that; they do not get it and they are stuck in their human density.

We here will continue to grow and feel and evolve our soul. We must remember we all have God in us- a little speck of perfection. That is –perfection to be revisited when we feel love. Transition implies moving from one stage to another-hopefully vertically and we need to tap into this perfection in us to move about from stage to stage. Moving about from stage to stage is remembering we have the perfection in us -that little piece of God and that propels us to begin our transition, knowing that we can in fact arrive. Arriving means that we have attained yet another level of existence and we visit it knowing we will be moving through another stage while staying first for a while in a " motel of mirrors", which I have repeated in the spirits' words to me in whatever form the learning is taking place on our path. Remembering all this will get us through whatever we charted, or even if we get off track, or in the breakdown lane, that speck of God is strong enough to pull us out and allow us to put ourselves back on track.

Spirits tell me futuristic things only rarely. Most people come to me at a pivot in their lives or at least a potential pivot, and if it is extremely important, they will impart information about what could occur. I insist that it is hard to totally know what is going to occur, as people exercise free will. Even if something is really charted, or destined the human may not follow the opportunity charted by the soul in its incipiency.

It is much easier to see with hindsight how spiritual our lives have been. Suddenly seeing that this particular person came into our lives at that particular time and we are at that particular place to have that particular experience is only available to most people when they arrive at the new other place on their path to evolvement.

When I worked in the retail store my ex and I shared, I used to watch people open or try to open the safe. Each staff member would at various times have major trouble opening the safe. He would go over to it. Sure he was turning it to the right properly hitting the number, and turning it to the left properly, knowing the combination by heart; everyone with surety would try to open the safe. Time after time , there would be the inevitable "Oh crap," the safe would not open. Attempt after attempt would take place even with the knowledge of the right combination. After sometimes three or four attempts the safe would finally be able to be opened. I liken that to our circumstances as humans. The spirits said to me that this is likened to the fact that we humans who house spirits all have the right combination to open the lock. Inside the safe is the soul or light contents- our real treasures. When a person finally after much frustration, opens the lock, there is an exhale. You know the combination to all the light and tools that you have. You are the safe and you have the combination to unlock it and find the treasure of tools inside you to become the highest being you were destined to be, and to use the tools that you have inside you to direct yourself and rely on yourself each step of the way.

The spirits say that there is order in the universe. The story will end the way it is supposed to end. Maybe in some person's case it takes more tries or maybe lifetimes but eventual completion of tasks is the goal here.

You have the right and the responsibility to be yourself. Push yourself beyond the periphery of who you are. We do not really have that much time to either pleasure ourselves or suffer that much in the life that only lasts about 80 years. The song that is my favorite is:

> *Where are you going my little one little one,*
> *Turn around and you're two*
> *Turn around and you're four*

Turn around and you're a young man going out of my door.[2]

The importance of this is that one needs to concur that time is short on this planet to be as loving, giving and cognizant of our soul's plans as we can be.

Hell. Hell is when your soul and your human are not in synch- when your human or ego inclusive of greed, envy, jealousy, over ambition, addiction, etc. rule over the soul. The soul's plans for you to manifest in this incarnation have become so separate from the ego's immature demands. There is a disconnect between soul and human. Hell is internal chaos. There is no hell over there. You want to get to the highest level that you can over there. But hell is actually here, in the form of internal disconnect, to which I allude , which is the soul disconnect from the ego. It is internal chaos, Do not worry it can be morphed. Your soul can get pushed too far from your human and there is a huge disconnect. Humans can get caught up in ego motives and aspirations which are superseding the lofty goals of the soul in its changed quest for evolution. The soul is impeded in its progress and can even go backwards. The soul struggles to fight with the personality but humans have a way of winning that fight for periods of time. One can nearly become soul-dead if the personality strangles the goals of the soul. The soul always lives and can be awakened thankfully at whatever time the ego –personality backs away a bit.

Fear. Fear can be looked at as helpful. Fear can be a motivator; you should never be in a relationship where you feel fear. So when you feel fear it is a barometer, an indicator that you should get out. So even if you are in a negative situation and fear comes in, whether it is a light

[2] Song and lyrics by Kingston Trio and Harry Belafonte in 1959.

fear like "Oh he's cheating on me, and I must leave" or "I think I she is secretly taking money from me"- whatever it is, whatever the fear is that is an indicator. It is not that there should not be any; it is that you should get out, and you are motivated to change. Look at negative emotions as traffic lights; caution, stop, and change. If anyone has ever sat in traffic, they know that the light does turn green.

Fear as a need which propels you is pretty interesting; fear can obviously move you to do different things, go beyond the periphery of what you were the minute before the fear happened. Listen to your body, your body can talk to you. If you feel butterflies in your stomach in a yucky way sometimes that can really be bad. You can feel if you try what you feel in a particular situation. Always remember there is order in the universe, even if you do not see it completely. You might only see a piece of it, it is part of a master plan. One thing is always certain, there is always change. If you feel fear it is time to change something. Your human must get you out of a situation that has become desperate. Once again to be in movement and not stuck, let your fear help and propel you forward into metamorphosis.

We have to look at our lives by not looking to the left or right of us. When I was at the beach, they pointed out the people building sand castles. You do not look at how the person to your left is building a fish, or the person to the right is building a fort with upside down buckets. The point is that you build your own sand castle. There is no perfect sand castle. If it starts falling apart, you add whatever amount of water you want. Feel what it feels like to feel the sand and that feels perfect because it feels what it feels like to you. However your mound of sand works is yours. If it falls apart and you just want a pile of sand that is okay. Add water ,feel the texture play with it as you want, feel whatever you are creating with the sand and water mixture. Build it in whatever way you want again. It is like your life. It may fall apart like parts of your life. It is what it is. Enjoy parts of your process. You have water and sand in whatever structure you have made. It is your structure like your life. It is beautiful because it is yours. The mixture that you make, the amount of water that you put in the sand to make it the texture you need to build what you want, is your perfect combination of water and sand. So if you end up just building a mound of sand to the perfect texture to your fingers while you are sitting in the sun that day is your perfect sand castle. Do not worry about what the kid beside you is making for his sand castle or that adult is making for her sand castle; your sand castle is perfect for you.

They told me that we need to want our neighbor's dreams to come true to have your own come true. If everyone wished each other well we would all have somebody praying for us and concentrating on us and giving us energy. So everything could work out for the best. I do not think that is a contradiction to the concept of a chart. I believe it merely is suggesting that the quickest route from point A to point B can be attained and or plan A is the one which is employed with added extra energy focused to it.

I look at a tree, I see the tree in front of me but under the tree are the roots in the ground, all interwoven. Some roots are dying .Some are absorbing nourishment to feed the tree. All of our lives are like the tree. We feed each other, but our lives are full of winding roads and processing of all sorts of scenarios, directions, paths, and branches of our inner selves. We do not immediately see which of our roots are hurting us or helping us and where exactly we are going. It is much easier with hindsight to see how spiritual our lives have been, to suddenly see that this person came into our own lives to bring us to that place to have that experience to continue our path. It is only available to most people when they arrive at another place. The bottom line is that you are a tree standing, you are on the ground, you are rooted. You are standing with all the underpinnings in the complicated roots. Some are nourishing you, and some of the toxins are going to fall off. You are a tree, strong, alive, here, nourished by the spirits, nourished by other humans in certain ways, and you must not let anyone knock you down. You do not have to anyway!

The spirits told me one day I was to enjoy myself. I was to listen to others slowly and really have a chance to hear what people were saying. The spirits told me that I better get used to it- that the one thing that is immutable in life is that it always changes. They reminded me that when I was a kid we used to play ball outside, and shout to the other kid, "Ready or not here it comes!" That is how they want me to understand life. Ready or not here the change or curve or challenge comes!

The spirit that I communicate with is the manifestation of the mix of the soul and the human. He has landed on the other side or transitioned and the form that is shown to me is the part of the personality of the human superimposed on which is the wisdom of being a soul. I therefore can glean the person himself as well as the understanding delivered to me of the insight and evolvement in the spiritual realm.

The dead spirits on the other side come through whether they have been dead for days or decades. Sometimes they just want to say hi- that they are okay and have watched you do something like some mundane housely chore. I have had spirits come through and merely

28

say that you squashed strawberries in a blender and had a totally uncharacteristic lunch of that mixed with apple juice today as well as giving profound life-changing substance to a receiving hopeful person sitting before me.

Your heart carries all your strength. The key is, the question still remains what is exactly charted and what you have free will over. The question is answered, I think, by the fact that you have plan A, B and C. Like I said, you have the quickest way you can transform and then there are the not so quick ways .It is important to remember it is never about you-just the human .It is about how your pact with your soul and the universe enter the scene. It is between you and all the people you have ever been. It is about you and how you give unconditional love. That is the main purpose for why we are here. I was told that when you cross over you are going to be asked what you think you accomplished here. If your answer is "I have this suitcase filled with cash ,"they will merely repeat the question .Money is okay as a tool but it is beside the point in terms of after life angel points. Any forgiveness you exude whether for yourself or for another is between you and God not you and the one being forgiven. Unconditional love reigning is the goal. Becoming as high as you can on the continuum of learning what you set out to accomplish wins you many more accolades on the other side than any praise of a human.

There is no better than, there is no less than. I do not see it coming when there are arguments down here, when people get so mad and get hung up on really small petty issues, but you can not judge that. Honor the spirits' wisdom that love is key and honor yourself and others always. Peace would be nice. I float from the world of chaos to peace as often as I can. Feel empowered. We are all part of the universe and working together.

Maybe the universe has planned that we all elevate our vibrations and morph as one big unit comprised of all of us parts and the planet will take off to a higher vibration!!

CONTINUUM

WE ARE ALL ON THE CONTINUUM OF SOUL EVOLVEMENT.

It is important to remember as the spirits told me one day that we are on a continuum. The continuum can be viewed as a line of growing or soul evolvement. It must be remembered that we were all or will at sometime be at these points on the path of evolvement, so we must not judge anyone on the continuum because you are really judging yourself. We are all moving. Some parts of the unit are farther along in the learning process than others. When you forgive someone his place, you are actually forgiving the time when you were in that space because guaranteed you were or will be at some point in the eternal soul.

When you forgive somebody, you are actually forgiving yourself because we are all on a continuum of understanding and soul growth. If you condemn someone else, it is ridiculous because you have been there, done that or you are about to. So when you forgive someone you forgive yourself and the road remains open.

When you do not forgive someone, you carry it. It is not condoning what they did, it is merely unblocking you. If you experience it, it will feel different than thinking it. When you really understand that we are all part of the same scheme ,the paradigm changes. It frees you up. People have different time frames. It is far more productive to work on your own issues than to focus on how you cannot change others.

It is very hard to understand why you cannot tweak this or that to make your relationship work or work better, but you cannot do something to which another person is not receptive; it is fruitless to fight the resistance of another person's mindset. People have different types of feelings. It might just be on your chart; you are following it and it is your time to look forward and morph. Your challenging soul mate may have charted growth time later on, or may be going off chart. It is possible to do that.

If you feel that you are not connected hop back on the continuum line. The spirits are here to help us. The more you evolve on the continuum the better off you will be the next time you try. I think it can be likened to bumper guards on a bowling alley ,to which I have previously alluded. The quickest way to grow or score is straight down the alley, but if someone gets side tracked or off the mark, the bumper guards are put in place to put him back on. In translation that may mean that he goes through experiences that exaggerate his problem offering him the chance to see up close and personal where he is falling off the mark. A human always has free will, so when I do a reading and they want to know what will happen in the future, I might only say something if the spirits want me to, but free will may deter someone from following the shortest route to growth. Therefore, he may not appear at the right time for the right thing to happen. I would say this is plan A, alternative plans B and C also exist. So you will be offered and you probably will accomplish what you need to accomplish, but human density can take somebody very far off course and they definitely will zigzag their way to where they need to be, taking much more time. With only 80 years on this planet potentially, it is not that much time to do what you need to do

I would certainly do what rewards one with the greatest growth in the time allowed on this earth, so as to advance as far along the continuum as possible.

CANTER

THE GOAL IS TO HAVE HARMONY BETWEEN THE SOUL AND THE EGO.

When I was horseback riding, the spirits told me about what was happening. They told me that it was amazing that I, a 124 pound being could actually control the 1400 pound horse. They said that the horse represents the soul or universe if you prefer. It may in fact be an illusion that the horse or the universe really allows you to control it. It is that when you are riding in a beautiful canter, that is what it looks like and feels like when your soul is working in harmony with your human. It is smooth and coordinated and feels light, gliding, and connected. When you are on the continuum and you are riding beautifully;you might be thrown off because you were not hanging on. Then when you let people trample you and you get thrown off the continuum you have let people or situations pull you in other ways and you are off track. You are off the continuum or your track if you are reacting to people who pull you and are only a pile of reactions. Do not let them push you around anywhere they want. Gain as much control as you can of your life again. Anybody has the potential to be picked up and guided back.

The horse decides to let the human ride it. It is cooperation. The horse seemingly lets you go left and lets you go right or fast or slow. The horse is likened to the soul or interchange the word universe. The human is the human or ego. The ultimate point is to have harmony with the ego and the soul just like the cooperation of the horse and its rider. It is beautiful to watch and or be part of the harmony that happens in the canter. It is kind of hard to believe the horse is not aware of this whole thing. Everything in the synchronicity is working in harmony of the ego and the soul. When the soul has communicated to the human what it needs and the human receives the information and acts properly it is a smooth ride. The right path is really the smoothest ride .It is the quickest plan to soul evolvement- the quickest path from point A to point B.

So is there an illusion that the person is really riding the horse or the universal soul or is the soul represented by the horse, letting the rider think he is doing it? Or is it a balance? I guess in the final analysis, we all should balance our human and our soul or universe together in the perfect soul canter, and that is when we are doing things right.

When the cantering is smooth and connected, things like the following happen as they did in my family. How various couples formed is interesting.

When my mother graduated college, her friend Sarah started a preschool. She needed some help and asked my mother who was her best friend for years, to be an assistant. My mother said sure, even though it was not her field. They creatively and warmly cared for the young children. A little boy named Paul took a particular liking to my mother. Everyday when his mother picked him up, the two would share the events of the day. The woman, who eventually became my aunt, suggested to my mother that she might like my aunt's brother in law. My mother hesitated a little, but upon hearing of the accolades of this person, finally consented. They went out on their blind date and really liked each other. After two weeks, my father suggested "Would you like to get engaged?

because if you don't somebody is going to fix me up with someone from the next town." But he was gentler than it sounds, and she was overtaken by her affection for him already and was not sure what to do and verbalized that. She said " I really like you, but it's kind of soon. I don't really want you to go out with anyone else, but...." He responded "Well, just try being engaged to me and see if you like it. If you don't like it, you don't have to be. Let's just see." They did get engaged and married and stayed a happy couple for fifty years.

This is a song that my mother in her beautiful voice, sang to my father, and what he felt about my mother. If a human being could write this song than it is possible for it to be true for you or anyone else.

> *...far beyond forever you'll be mine.*
> *I know I never lived before {in this body }(my words)*
> *And my heart is very sure*
> *No one else could love you more.*[3]

My second son was friendly with two teenaged boys in high school. They were brothers born a year apart. They had a relationship from September to December. Then on Christmas vacation, they were going to a movie and the brothers asked if they could bring their sister along since she was home on her college vacation. My son said "Sure, why don't I bring my big brother who is also home on his college vacation". The five of them went and had a great time. The two college kids paired up, within months were engaged and married soon after that. My second son and the brothers went their separate ways after that. It

---

[3]The music was written by Riz Ortolani and Nino Oliviero, Marcello Ciorciolini provided the Italian lyrics and this was adapted into English by Norman Newell.

seems like their souls had this contract to bring the other two souls to meet and it was finished after that. Mission accomplished.

For my brother's 44thish birthday, my sisters played a joke and decided to put an ad in a magazine for their socially unreaching brother. Several women responded to his ad, one of which was a wonderful reaching creative lady, who within two years, married him .They are still happily married after 15 years.

When I had a New Years Eve party in the late 60's, which for me was very uncharacteristic, I invited about 20 friends. One of these friends was a platonic friend and I told him to bring a friend. I assumed he would bring a female date. I was in my playroom in the cellar, when this guy walked down the stairs followed by another male. I looked at this second young man and I suddenly had this impression in my mind that " I am going to marry this man". A couple of years later, I did. We were married for over two decades.

Throughout high school my third son and now girlfriend, never really crossed paths. They were in a class of 300, both took honors courses and shared some mutual friends. Amazingly it was not until the weekend before graduation that they met. They sat at the same table for an honor society inauguration- he with his father and she with hers. Her father asked a lot about my son, she gave him the little information that she knew – but mainly that he was smart. Time passed and they met again. A friend had called her at around 10pm one night saying that he was going to a concert in Washington D.C. and he had extra ticket because his friends had bailed last minute, they were leaving the next morning before dawn. Typically she would not even have fathomed asking her father for permission to go on an over night road trip with two boys, out of the question. Maybe if she had at least a month to mentally prepare him for the event she might be able to go. For some reason unbeknownst to her, my son's name was the key to the lock and she was allowed to go. Her father had remembered him from the honor society dinner and somehow my son gave him a good impression. She went on the trip with my son and their friend. She enjoyed conversations with my son and it was a fun trip. After only seeing him briefly at a restaurant in the next two years, at a large annual local Feast she ran into their mutual friend who took them on the trip and she asked about my son . He said he is right over there. She went up to him gave him a big hug (with the help of a little wine), said some words and kindly saved his phone number in her phone. She did not think much of it at the time; often at this event you run into people and talk about how you should hang out, but never do. A couple of days later while she was sitting in her cubicle at her engineering internship, bored, on a Tuesday, not looking forward to the week ahead, he called. She rarely picks up for a phone number she doesn't recognize, especially at work, but she did. It was my son asking if she wanted to go out that night. She spent the rest of the day nervous and excited, with no need. They hit it off really well and are currently continuing their adventure together. It has been almost 5 years.

My sister owned a successful three person company. After getting to know my sister, her female employee suggested to her brother, to call my sister to go out on a date.

He called the office one day and introduced himself, and pretended to have a company. He wanted to commission the firm to create a logo. Upon learning who he was, my sister thought he was interested in a free logo and referred him to someone else. There was something he liked about her though, and he called again and he told her he would fax information to her about his company. She said fine, but when the fax came through in a couple of days, she discarded it. He called again and seemed somewhat in earnest, and she said that if he faxed it to her again at that moment - she would look at it while they were on the phone. He did, they chatted and then she excused herself because she had a situation about her horse. He said he loved riding and he would really like to meet her in person. Through a series of a few missed meetings and rescheduled dates, they finally met and quickly there after fell madly in love with each other. They have remained so for 17 years. At their wedding, his sister made a speech in which she said " I ended up having a sister in law, whom I would have chosen to be my friend in life .

A HUMAN CAN GO
OUT OF BODY

OTHER VIBRATIONS CAN HELP YOU MORPH

On a serious note, I was madly in love with this woman that I will call Maggie . She had arrived at my store that my ex-husband and I had in search of a job as a sales floor worker .With clear hindsight , I could see the path of props used as stepping stones to our soul growth. My co-manager and I had just finished talking about the fact that if any girls come in the store we needed to hire one due to the imbalanced ratio of males to females. This number changes on a fairly constant basis due to the ever changing flow of the staff. I barely knew her in the store, but after my ex husband removed me from the company, she sought me out and we began a relationship.

I did not even know that a person could really fall in love with someone of the same sex, but it is entirely an option for maybe soul and karmic situations. We struggled through several years of dissention after two years of phenomenal bliss and connection. It became a lopsided relationship. There were lots of different factors. I still wanted to make it work; I was so fascinated by and drawn to her.

What was interesting was I heard there was a psychic in town who was also a medium . I had gone to her years and years earlier right after Adam died, never knowing that I was going to become even near her vibrational level. I want to honor all psychics and I want to honor people's belief in them. Sometimes I find that people's accuracy can greatly vary. This particular person I trusted, and was quite delighted I could go see her . She was going to lead a church service as well as offer private readings during the few days she was going to visit from another state. I called her up and said " Please Crystal can you give me a reading?" She remembered me since I had seen her a couple of times in the interim of 15 years from the time that my friend Adam had died and now .I went over to see her and explained how I am so completely in love with this woman but it had seemed economically imbalanced, emotionally imbalanced and we were fighting all of the time. After the first two years of bliss I questioned what happened in these last 6 years ?I was trying and trying to make amends. I did not want to lose the magnificent feeling that I had in the beginning. What could I possibly do to make this work? And she smashed me between the eyes for a minute, symbolically and she said "You can't! You can't do it! There can be metamorphosis but both parties have to want to do it." She insisted that I can not change her. I can only change me and all the things I wanted to change about my mate I was powerless to do and we just were not going to make it in this lifetime.

The overwhelming affirmations that I know I have incarnated with her about 17 times, helped me persist in my longings for her. Every time we made love it was phenomenal and many times in the beginning I flipped into past life regressions and I would see her and me in different persons but I knew it was she and I. I had seen us as Indians, English women, various sexes, various times.

There were times when we made love when she would have seen something in silence, and when we talked about it later I had seen what she had seen. One time she was visiting mountains and they were very special and sacred to her and I started talking with her saying "Oh those mountains were great." That part was wonderful but there was a tremendous imbalance in the relationship as it progressed. I felt that I was more of a giver, but that was just my opinion. What was interesting was that Crystal was saying that my friend was not going to change in this lifetime so that we could be together. I was there engaged in hopeful anticipation of a positive resolution to my situation for a couple of hours.

What was equally fascinating was after the reading Crystal and I took a brief walk and she was the only other person with whom I could take a walk who could see the same spirits. Beside a tree we saw a little boy digging in the sand and then there was a little girl outside of her house. They were spirits and we shared that common intuition or communication from the other world, or maybe we traveled to another dimension together but we saw the same things whatever it is.

I was unresolved that night .I attempted to go to bed. During that night I was restless .My feet were just going up and down and up and down as if I were walking. I had my eyes closed and I sort of thought I was asleep but I was always awakened by my feet moving up and down and completely unresolved thinking "Why can't it work?" In the morning I called Crystal and asked " Please I know you are here for only one more day but I have to go to the retail store where I work this morning but please can I see you this afternoon ?" She laughed and said "I knew you were going to call Sue, because you came to me last night." She was three towns away and I said "What do you mean by that?" She said "You were pacing in my room all night and you told me why you and Maggie were not together.

This kind of visit or traveling can happen, but not that frequently. I have only had four nighttime visitations by souls like yours in all the years I have been doing readings. I will tell you this afternoon exactly what your soul told me during the night, and I'm exhausted and I am going to rest. I'll see you later on at two o'clock."

I pulled up to the church, went inside to see her and she said "Susan, you told me that you and Maggie have been together since Egyptian days and you were males and you were about 12, a young boy who had inherited land. Maggie was much older than you and she was a male tax collector. He told you that you had to give him a certain amount of money to keep your land and at the same time he was actually very fond of you. He was gay, and he took you under his wing into his home, and you became lovers. You fell madly in love with him, but nothing you ever did was quite good enough. You felt this and when you got a few years older, he took on another young man and booted you out. You committed suicide over Maggie who was then that man." She told me "If you ever do that you're protected from it ever happening again, at least when a lover commits suicide over another lover." In this lifetime it made perfect sense because there was some money exchange that should not have been there even if it concerned only borrowing or helping with day to day living expenses. I always felt like I was not good enough for her, even though I certainly was. I felt like nothing was going to please her, and allow me to have the feeling that she would stay with me in this lifetime . Nothing was going to make the situation now change for us unless, as Crystal said, she did a past life regression and went back to those days or lives when the scenario existed. The interesting thing was, I asked Crystal " Why did we have that set up in the first place? Why do we continue lifetime after lifetime with the same theme?" She said " Because this is your opportunity to break it. The good news is if you do break that theme then healing can take place, and if Maggie had realized where her place was in a past life regression, she might have accepted you and understood your love for her and things could evolve. She could see herself as a victimizer and then things could change."

Once again, two parties have to want to make something work and then if you do some healing work (which I have done and continue to do) and some work with the spirits, metamorphosis can happen. I still have hope that the imperfections that I manifested in that relationship and the imperfections that she manifested in that relationship could dissipate.

I know that lessons are always a two-way street. I clearly had some sort of self-esteem issue that Maggie as her soul had offered to challenge me with; and the ultimate test of unconditional love was part of this scenario. I know I passed that test because I never stopped caring for her and have not yet. I think about her oftentimes and there is no substitute for her thus far .If we each learn whatever was charted here, we could change and morph in a minute and be lovers again, but we will see. She is off with another and I as you see, have been freed up to write my intuitions down in this body of words and grow as a soul unimpeded by the ambiguity of that previously absorbing scenario. I know that in the quiet place is where I love her still......

The fascinating thing in that true episode of my life is that I think people can have their souls travel out of their body and some people might call this astral traveling. I believe that your soul is attached to you by some sort of chord, and maybe that is made up of energy as well. So you are not going to get lost, but you can travel to other vibrations, and I think in that vibration is where you are meeting the other soul and your souls have conversations. It could be that there is a similarity when my soul and a deceased person's soul meet halfway. There has to be a place which is literally a vibrational dimension, where we sort of hover over the dense vibration of human bodies.

It is fascinating. I can tell you it is real to the people who experience this phenomenon. It can be healing if you allow it and you can morph in a minute, when you have an A HA! moment from an experience from the spirits .They are loving and they want to help. We are all capable of changing our vibration, but there has to be desire to elevate and probably belief in the fact that you can elevate your vibrations, kind of like switching the TV channel- you can morph in a minute by switching the channels. When you switch the channels you can receive communication from the spirits, which is very didactic. Pay attention because there are a lot of lessons that you can learn, and you turn to those who watch over you as you progress in this body.

MORPH

ONE DAY I RODE AN AMBULANCE WITH MY MOTHER FOR ONE OF HER MINI STROKES. WE WERE THERE TOGETHER AND SHE HAD AWAKENED AND MY SISTER ARRIVED INTO THE ROOM. SHE SAID TO MY 85 YEAR OLD MOTHER, " DO YOU FEEL YOURSELF?" MY MOTHER REPLIED, "NOT REALLY, BUT ACTUALLY," SHE ADDED, "I GUESS I DO BECAUSE THIS IS WHO I AM RIGHT NOW." THE SPIRITS SUGGEST THAT CHANGE CAN OCCUR FROM MINUTE TO MINUTE (IT IS NOW THREE YEARS LATER AND SHE IS DOING FINE).

RIDE AN ELEPHANT.

I scratch down what is filtered to me and put up wisdom on paper plates on my fridge all the time. I can be doing anything but usually spirits tell me things during a walk or during the wee hours of the morning and certainly deep tools for living come through in each reading. Some of them I will share with you here.

Forgive someone today. When you forgive someone you are actually forgiving yourself a la the continuum. It also frees up your soul. You are not condoning the behavior of the person who bothered you. It is more that you do not carry the rock on your shoulder of thinking about it on a constant basis and it dragging you down. You have to really feel that, however it just cannot be words. You have to understand to the bottom of your toes why you are forgiving. It is never about the other person. It is to get you unstuck. You can morph and begin to feel light and possibility again.

Do Not Judge. Now do not judge who you are and anyone else for who they are right now. This is just who you are right now on the continuum. Next minute you can be different. You can change in a minute away from what you are right now. The next minute does not have to be dictated by your past even a minute before this minute. Change things.

Realize you cannot judge anyone. We are all on certain points on a continuum. We are all humans together. We even fluctuate ourselves. You might have done that which is upsetting you beyond your ability to cope you may think. You may have done that - or maybe will in some future time. All humans are somewhere on the continuum. He is in a certain place on the continuum of soul evolvement. So are you. Forgiveness is key. Forgive someone today. You will feel lighter. When you forgive someone, you are actually forgiving yourself for being there at sometime in your life or lives. It does not condone his behavior. You are forgiving him for being human. So basically you are forgiving yourself for being human. We all have every degree of the continuum in our selves. All souls are the same potentially. We are all manifesting different levels of the continuum. Even the biggest .great gurus sometimes get annoyed. That is okay. You are not stuck trying to change someone, you are recognizing they are human and so are you. When you recognize that it is just one line of spiritual evolution we are on, we are on the same line at some point. It is key when you forgive them when they lapse back . Everyone has a certain amount of growth. By forgiving you move forward. You need to understand and participate in the understanding that everybody deals with things in different ways. Everybody has different amounts of growth. When you forgive them you are forgiving yourself too. We are all manifesting at different levels on this continuum of soul evolvement. Forgive someone . You are not then trying to change someone or undue what had been done. You cannot control anyone. When you recognize it is just one line of challenges and how they are dealt with varies, you are free to move forward on your path immediately leaving what happened behind you.

Change up what you do. If you go to a certain variety store all the time go to another one. If you eat roast beef every Tuesday eat pizza. Ride an elephant. I rode an elephant at the age of 58 when the circus came to town. Go beyond the periphery of who you thought you were. You get the idea. Change the routine you have established in terms of the day to day activities you have done for years.

Your place is where you are right now. Your emotions today do not have to dictate what your emotions are going to be tomorrow. You can choose in the next minute to feel something different.

If you had or are having a bad day put it behind you and be ready to embrace the new minutes about to unfold. Embrace the life that you are being given this minute.

Your place is where you are right this minute. It is where you are. That is all you have. You can go anywhere you want from here.

You can morph in a minute by knowing in the next minute of your life, everything could change. You could get an insight or bump into someone that will give you the hug you want.

Face the music. When you are involved in something you do not like, feel what it is you feel and then move on to the next thing. To grow up, face the music and move on. When you are involved in something you do not like, morph and move on from it. It is very difficult, you have to experience things, but you can experience them as if you are watching on a movie screen. Move on to something that makes you feel good, instead of staying stuck in something that does not make you feel good. That does not mean avoid thinking about it and working through it because it will still be there if you do not work through it. Work through it and simultaneously stand beside it or even hold the troublesome experience by the hand and walk forward because it will not go away, so just walk with it into the future. Move into the flow of things on to the next thing. You may find the universe hugs you. You may find that it has you on a path leading you more closely to your goal. The future is even in the next minute, not the next two weeks. Morph in a minute by taking your terrible feelings with you, and once you are moving everything will morph.

You are not alone. Know that there are many souls around you all the time. They are behind you, they can not manipulate you. Go forward knowing you are not alone-that can change you in a minute. I give you blessings, wish you peace and I wish you the knowledge that you really need to know you are loved no matter what happens in this life. The spirits love you, the spirits are with you, you are a pile of energy and energy stays alive, energy transforms, you can always, if you take the responsibility, do it. Expect today to be filled with love for you from somebody, anybody, it does not matter. Keep trying, you have got nothing better to do. For instance, I watched a seagull attempting to get a fish and he kept swooping down, missing. Then on about the eighth try he came up with the fish. Do not worry about it, even though he did not get the first fish he kept trying and then succeeded.

Know that there are spirits watching over you and you are not alone. Angels , your deceased relatives ,friends and pets are there . I have this affirmed on a daily basis in my readings. It is hard not to have them in the physical body for sure, but they watch and whisper to you. You will see them sometime. They look down on you and you will be able to bridge the gap through a reading now or when you cross over later on.

You need to know the universe has a plan. You do not necessarily know what it is. You need to realize that you cannot control another person or the outcome of a circumstance. You have to keep on going. You do not control another person. Keep on breathing, eat something you like, and keep walking .Put one foot in front of the other. Keep moving. The universe has a plan to end things the way they are supposed to end. That may mean that it will end differently than your desire is at the moment when you do not see the weaving or the roots of the tree like I told you. Sometimes, like the song says, unanswered prayers can be wonderful. The spirits tell me the universe is always, every minute, working. You are a participant, you try hard and that is important, and try hard to understand that the universe has its ways. Another insight is that almost nothing is impossible. I phrase it in that way, because like the unanswered prayers you might not get exactly what you want, but anything can happen.

Tools are helpful. I do not believe a person can just let something go, I think you need tools. Change your life up. Shake things up. Change what you do. It is okay to have an emotion but do not live there. Keep remembering that life keeps moving. This feeling you have, good or bad, it will not last. It cannot stop you. The flow continues. Know that you are part of life flow. The world can open up to you if you give it a chance. Have the feeling that you can do things. Have hope that the next minute will be better than this. You never know. Your next minute does not have to be dictated by your past moments. You can change. Remember all the glorious possibility inside. Even the possibility that there is something else should wake up your sleeping soul and give you some hope. You can also start picking up on the intuition you may be having from the spirits. You hopefully will say at the end of a day that you were productive not that you lost a day of your time. A little step forward is fine. It does not have to be a leap. A change in perspective can be a precursor to movement. I watched a bird in a tree once. He was sitting a top the tree looking down at all things. He stayed for quite some time. Then he flew away. Sometimes that is okay too, to make no moves, and just think, assessing the situation.

Blame equals quicksand. In life you can stay bitter, or move from that and get better. You can jump back in the stream of the universe flowing .Jump on the continuum and find yourself wherever you are and evolvement can be jumpstarted. Anger and love can not exist in the same place. Getting stuck in rage and blame and bitter regrets can likewise take the place of growing or movement. It is like the bumper guards on the bowling alley. If you get stuck and are not aiming for your goal, they can bounce you back on-if you let them. Remember our energy always moving and can transform from one state to another. Death is like ice cubes to water as we said. Living can be everything from a bit of transformation to major overhauls. Whatever our challenges are they are to be overcome; our weaknesses are never to be hidden behind or used as excuses. They are to be overcome.

Blaming somebody else is not going to have you morph. If you blame somebody else it keeps you stuck in calling yourself a victim. You have got to realize the only one who is making you a victim is you, most of the time. Think of yourself as the tree again, you are strong, you are standing. Your knees are not jelly, you are standing, you are alive. Because of that you have chance to change, and there are so many people on the other side in spirit form who have your back, they love you. Do not feel alone. Remember you are not alone; you have souls behind you, with you walking. I have had so many affirmations that souls watch you everyday. They can not tell you what to do; they can whisper hunches in your ear. You picture quicksand, where you could be stuck forever. Then picture the ocean beside it where you can swim out infinitely to an always exciting ever changing future. You pick. Remember blame equals quicksand.

Do not beat yourself up or anyone else. They are all instrumental in your growth or in your opportunity to grow. You see opportunity exists to grow constantly-to morph. Right now you may not know where you are headed. Just do your best in each moment. Do what is happening right now to the best of your ability and sensitivity. Then you will see to what it leads. You should not be attached to an outcome that you can not see. Every step is significant. It is fine because if you are in a challenging situation, guess what? You can frame it as an opportunity to grow and you are evolving without even trying to ask for a challenge. Remember ready or not here it comes! Also remember that the statement that we are humans is an illusion. We are souls in a human body, therefore anything is possible. Souls are from the other world and therefore have the power to do the better than human things. Just about anything is possible.

You have no idea the significance that you have to somebody else, but choose to be as loving and caring and forgiving as you can, every minute. As you do that to other people you are really doing it for yourself. This is because I think that when you are loving, it is going to be in a higher vibration and ultimately the chance of love coming to you is higher .It is kind of like if you go out in your day and you are angry angry angry, probably you are going to attract somebody angry. That might be okay if you are facing issues and it will show you how angry you are, but the ticket is always getting out of disconnect or disconnected feelings.

It is your unique path. What you must remember is that it is your path. No matter what happens, do not let anyone tell you that you need to follow theirs. It is your path, your life, you are unique. There is no one else on your path, rejoice about that. It is going to have ups and downs and its good times and bad times, but nothing lasts forever. Even in the bad times, know that it is your route. Remember the tree, you do not know what is nourishing and what is going to die from your path, but toxins are being eliminated as well as new input is coming in to give you growth.

Remember in your life the spirits say answer to no one but yourself. You should try to please the person in the mirror. If you are on the right track, when you look in the mirror you are going to see beauty. You will notice that if you meet someone, his energy is high who is attuned, who is respecting the universe, who feels very alive. It is a person with whom you want to have contact and a person who recognizes that her soul is in flow with her person.

53

Her personality is in the right flow and place that her soul intended.

Answer to no one. It is your path. Do not let anyone veer you off it. Do not let them tell you they have the right way to be. You are beautiful. You have the freedom and the responsibility to be your own keeper of your own dreams and aspirations. Dream big as they say. Honor yourself. Take after yourself. As long as you are on the connective continuum of human cantering with the universe or soul in an attempt to love, better yourself and your part of the world. You are unique. There is no one else that is on your particular path. Rejoice. You are you enough .No one else can write your story but you.

Do not waste your energy. Do not keep spending the energy you have in directions where there is no return. Instead of feeling the inevitable flat feeling you will get, put your energy where you feel filled up. Aim in directions where there is return.

Learn from your enemy. Look at what you really do not like in your enemy. Reframe it. For instance, if you think he has more money than you and you resent it, look at how he got his money. Maybe he focused, was unchanging, and got educated. Maybe you should see where you could redo a part of your life using what he did. You do not have to do what he did with his money if that is what you do not like. Reframe how you look at your life and circumstances and change the way you look at what your enemy is doing. Maybe you are mad at yourself as much as him for your lack of doing what you really could be doing. So look at your enemy and see if there is anything he is doing that you could use.

Be grateful. You morph by feeling grateful for what you have. It is like the lady said "You get what you get and you don't get upset." Sure you get upset, you can get mad, but you let it go, you move on and know that there might be something better around the corner. There is hope. Not that you have to feel blame, but you did chart this for yourself. It is hard to believe, but there was this lady who I talked to years and years ago. She was one of the first ladies with whom I spoke of spirituality. She was a customer at the store at the time my ex and I ran it and she told me that the way you have to look at life is if you are walking on the street and a plant pot from the second story falls and hits you on the head, you asked for it. Personality did not ask for it, your soul asked for it.

Use what you have. One day I was in the store and I saw a man in his wheelchair smiling away and moving his arms to maneuver not asking assistance for anything. It was amazing to ponder about how many people do not use all their potential, with two arms two legs and ability to maneuver with ease mentally and physically wherever they want to go, but do not do life to their full potential-whereas this man who was handicapped was living up to his full potential.

To feel better when you are stuck, always remember there is somebody worse off. They remind me when I am hurting and I see someone in a wheel chair. Even though their scheme may look less than magnificent , it does not mean they are less evolved. Very often they are more evolved as a soul. But it makes me feel good that I have two legs and two arms and I can walk, and it makes me grateful. And that may in fact be one of their purposes. A person in a wheel chair may be contracted to do that; just to be there to remind us, a weak soul who is not as strong as they are, who is not making the most of the potential that they have to be reminded that they have got to use what they have got and what they have, to get whatever they need.

Realize that you have the power in your life. You are not the definition other people see you as. You define yourself in the moment that you can say "I can be whatever I want, because it is already inside me." You can morph in a minute and be different in the next minute than you are now. Your place is where you are. Because you are wherever you are this minute but next minute your place could be defined very differently. You can go anywhere you want to from here.

Mold the day like it is clay. Mold the day, go out and smile at somebody. Mold yourself like clay. Just feel like there is going to be a better day, that you have all this unmanifested power to interact in the world, with all the gifts that you have. Do not worry that your mother did not see it, that your father did not see it, that your lover did not see it. They are on their own paths. The bottom line is that you are a tree standing, you are on the ground, you are rooted. You are standing with all the underpinnings in the complicated roots. Remember, some are nourishing you, and some of the toxins are going to fall off. You are a tree, strong, alive, here, nourished by the spirits, nourished by other humans in certain ways, and you will not let anyone knock you down. You do not have to anyway.

Do not allow yourself to be judged. You can morph when you realize that you should not judge anyone, nor should they judge you. I do not know why humans have to attach labels to the plumbing of the pipes. It does not matter. I had a soul connection with a woman, and I have had a soul connection with a couple of men. It is almost a case by case basis and there are different lessons to be learned from different situations. You just love who you love and attraction between people comes because there are lessons to be learned in the situation. Whether you are black or white or gay or straight you are authentically you. Explore it and see what you are learning from it and morph into the best being you already have inside of you.

I do not believe in random occurrences. I am not sure that it matter whether you are wearing a red shirt that day, but it does matter how you interact with the humans with whom you experience your day. It does matter how you treat yourself. These things matter. I do not think it is random who you work with, mate with, who your children are. Your soul creates the scenario of your race, your color, your intelligence level. And do not forget that sometimes the person in the wheelchair that you see is a very advanced soul or the mongoloid child who is blissful is a very old soul. Someone who comes in to be abused on this level, must not be judged as if they are less evolved. Rather, the harder the tasks, very often, the more evolved one is. And on the other hand there is the dimension of souls who have struggled so and kind of earned a happy life this time, but it all balances.

Understand that no matter what you are going through, it will be resolved.

Ponder where you are going. A Doctor friend of mine once told me that if two people came to the office with the exact same complaint, he would give them the same treatment plan and comments. One would heal as of a few weeks later and one would not. Different things would account for that, he said, like someone who particularly was not getting any other attention at home, needed that focus for people to notice him. Some things occur because people need to slow down or speed up. Ultimately I think some ailments are just physical because we are, after all housed in imperfect bodies that can break a bit. Some ailments are spiritual because our perfect blueprint has broken down. Some things may occur because we charted them on our course. There really has to be a blend, therefore of physical and spiritual medicine. It makes sense. Take the frame from "Why me?" to "Where am I going from this diagnosis? What is this pointing out to me? What shall I do?" Nothing is not the answer. Life is what it is . We are moving and something will occur to us to keep moving past fear and pondering reasons for things. Metamorphosis will undoubtedly happen after a traumatic sickness.

It is okay not to be good at everything. You can morph when you realize you cannot be good at everything. Do not be hard on yourself . Another piece of who I am; my grandmother also used to walk, and I walk all the time. She was honored, when she was a school teacher and there are awards still given in her name for high academic achievement. However, she had no common sense. I am pretty much the queen of no common sense, even though I have sensitivities within other arenas. One of my sisters calls me Granny, which is what we called her. I remember one day, when I was about twelve my mother answered the telephone, and my grandmother had taken her usual walk. She called up because a storm came and it started to pour .My mother was responding "Oh okay fine." Then she looked at me and my two year old sister was standing by me. My mother was saying to her mother " I realize it started to rain, so I will come get you. Where are you?" My grandmother clearly looked and must have glanced up at the corner where she was standing in the downtown area. She looked up at the sign and came back to my mother and said "I'm at the corner of Walk and Don't Walk." She said this to my mother, my mother looked at me and shook her head, then she said "Well look at another street sign." And my grandmother said "Well I see one that says Junior St." My mother said "Don't move, I will find you." My mother said to me "Susan, can you watch your sister for a few minutes? I have to go downtown to pick up Granny." True story. So no matter how brilliant you are in certain readings, you are not in others .

Smile. Remember to smile at somebody for no reason everyday ,as this will snowball whether it is the waitress or the customer or the bank teller or your child or your mother. It will make two people happy. Not in any narcissistic sense, you are actually smiling at yourself , because we are all in this together and the raising of everyone's vibration actually raises yours also. We are one on this Spaceship Earth in a way, so if you laugh and smile the vibration can multiply. Everyone feels better as will you because you have just smiled at yourself. It is kind of like if you are good to someone you are good to yourself, the spirits say.

Short Tips.
Take a walk. You do not know what is going to happen on your walk; somebody might smile at you, you might be grateful that you have a body that can walk; you may get an insight if you could just get up and out. You can morph in a minute.

Life is feeding you. Sometimes you bite it and spit it out. Remember you can not change anybody, keep your chin up. You do not know what part you play in your life and sometimes in somebody else's.

I watched a movie of my 2nd son the other day as he was learning to walk. He was 11 months old. He fell and got up again. He fell and got up again. It shouted "Do not give up. Get up." He did like nothing had happened at all.

Do not let it take too long for you to be happy again when a part of you is broken.

Do not let it take too long to stay in the crap of today if you are miserable- please start to live again tomorrow.

Your emotions today do not have to be dictated by the emotions of yesterday or any moment before this.

If you need a miracle, be as much an amazing loving awakened soul to someone- anyone- that you can.

Right now you do not know where you are headed -just do what is happening now to the best of your ability and do not be attached to the outcome you cannot see.

Your heart carries all your strength.

Do not just react to people's provocations.

They told me that adversity offers training, Remember everything has a purpose. You see the tree standing . You do not see the roots. You do not see which are destroying the tree and which are nourishing it. It is necessary to trust that there are both.

Sometimes you just explode. Sometimes you just have to take a shit. Getting rid of the toxins is what you just have to do.

Listen slowly and harder to someone else. Life is hard for everybody.

To be free to follow the stairs one at a time is something you can only do if you do not focus on blame. Rest on your own knowledge that you are a soul encased in a human body always moving along the continuum of soul evolvement. The world can open up to you if you give it a chance. Have the feeling that you can do things.

Ready or not- here is another opportunity to grow.

Every time you work through some of your own baggage you leave some behind and you are able to move more lightly through the world.

They kiddingly one day said be a vegetarian do not devour humans. They mean by that I think do not drain energy when you need it off other humans; take it from the natural wonders like the sea ,the air and ideas.

There was a button that I saw in the store, it did not seem to have an author. It was something to the effect of "Live in the moment .uh oh it's gone!" You have got to take advantage.

If your ' horsepower' which is your universal power is low, the spirits told me your personality or human or ego has overtaken your soul, or its universal dictates . The human has to back off and let the soul gain its momentum and the self of the human should pull away or back and try to listen to the inner shouting of the soul to get back on track and feel the power of smooth cantering again.

You should have a pocket of power when you go to experience your day. Put in your pocket some energy you get only from the air and the water and the knowing of the plans of the universe-that it is in processing working order. Know that things will occur- that you will be pulled in the direction you need to keep growth a playing card in your life. Fill that day with power in your pocket .

They said you could visualize taking a pill of white light. —no chemicals- but a pile of power in the form of the pill of power.

I bet if someone offered to pay you to try to be happy or even nice, you people would try a lot harder.

To have a more filling life, if you are uncomfortable with something in your reality - change your reality. Many elements in your life can be morphed. Create a new normal.

A reading can morph you in a minute.

MY READINGS

I HAVE MY OWN LESSONS, SO
SOMETIMES I CANNOT READ MYSELF.
ONE DAY WHILE WALKING MY DOG,
WE GOT SKUNKED. I DID NOT SEE
THAT COMING.

The first time I became aware that I could read myself is a funny story. I always went down to the bridge near the village where I lived to feed the ducks and geese that nested there. On this one occasion, I drove down and did not have any bread, but needed to get eggs in the village anyway. I got out of the car and the geese came to greet me. I apologized profusely that I did not have any bread that day. The biggest goose faced me off, and as I kept apologizing, I started to walk across the street to get my eggs. The spirits said "Do not go get your eggs now". I wrestled with myself in my head and said "But I need eggs". So I proceeded to cross the street. The goose ran up behind me and bit me hard in the butt.

Another true silly story shows how small interesting things happen as well. I had met a girl and we were just going out for a little ride and we were going to walk by the beach. There was an ice cream shop near by and I did not know her that well, but we were both kind of lonely that day. We went over and we swung on the swings a little bit and I asked her " Do you want to go get some ice cream? I'll treat you ." It was a place with about 52 flavors and I looked at her and said " I think you are going to get butter crunch." She looked at me shocked and said "What are you? That's what I always get!" So fun things happen.

Being remiss about not having my teeth cleaned for a couple of years, I psychically had the inclination to call them on a random day off, Monday at mid morning, to see if they had any cancellations. They never really have any cancellations, and they were surprised at my request because immediately before I called - there was in fact a cancellation. This after a two week vacation in which their offices were closed, and they are usually inundated with work.

We had a snow storm, and I shoveled out the two spots we needed for the two cars that we park . A spirit said - shovel out a third spot because someone will show up. I looked at the foot of snow and thought twice, but honored the spirit and shoveled out the spot. Three hours later, an unexpected close friend from the past pulled up.

I went into the discount store that is near my home to buy flannel shirts for the approaching winter, and I had forty dollars in my pocket. I was really trying to change up my simple style of clothing as well as keep warm. I picked up four shirts, but then I had an intuition –"What if my son comes home soon, and wouldn't that be nice because he had moved to Boston a short time previously. I think I'll put one shirt back and buy him a package of underwear just in case he suddenly shows up." I went home with my bag and two hours later, he called and said "Mom, I am going to come home and visit in three days".

One day I was going home and got a call from a friend in the car who was stuck in a traffic jam. She called she said for some sane conversation. I responded to her comment about a sexual relations moratorium with her boyfriend with my comment about how it had been way too long- much longer a time in fact since I had had intimate relations and teasingly said that she and he should come over in my hot tub. I had never told her about my hot tub and I was not sure why I had at that moment. Then she exclaimed "Susan I am just starting to move a bit in the traffic and I am passing by a sign that reads 'hotel special- hot tubs at reduced price '"

I was talking to another friend on the phone and suddenly I started describing her way of hanging out in her room . I said " Your grandmother is here and she tells me you are lying in bed with your feet up and your legs crossed." She laughed and said she was. I continued that "There is a bird on your head. Also you have blanket up to your waist and are watching TV." She said " Yes I let my bird out of its cage and we are watching the TV."

I can now also sometimes tell what is going to happen on TV shows. I walked in and the show was on that the kids were watching and there was a teen-ager waiting to be picked up by her father at the bus station. I said that she was going to see her new step mother and the step brother and sister. The kids looked up at me as if I were crazy. Sure enough the divorced father, brought the teen-ager to a new neighborhood where the step wife was standing in front of the new house inside which were the new stepsiblings at the dinner table.

One day I when a bit lonely(still thinking about Maggie), decided to go to Newport and change my daily routine. As I headed out the front door, I grabbed my blue jacket. The spirits said 'No" you should switch it to the green jacket." I pondered for a minute that they were both the same weight and why should I switch . Knowing by now to listen, I replaced the blue jacket with the green. I drove a while and landed in Newport at about a quarter to 11. I got out of my car and started walking and then decided to return to the car to get my jacket. As I did, I noticed several groups of people all walking in the same direction and that someone in each group was wearing green. I thought to myself, " I'll follow them and if there is a green contest of some kind I can compete." I followed them in that direction and landed at a main street where there were hundreds of people gathered for a St. Patrick's Day parade. I am not Irish and it was a few days early, but a wonderful way to spend my lonely day. I fit right in and enjoyed the two hour long festivity. I remembered that my sister-in-law had a piece of work in the art museum in Newport and decided to go see it. I randomly sauntered around ,went to the bathroom , got a snack, and started walking up the hill to the museum. I went in and paid admission, and walked around meandering looking at various art works and went upstairs and downstairs in the various rooms. I then upon not seeing her name beside any work, asked at the place where I purchased admission if there were another part of the museum I did not see yet. She said "Yes, across the courtyard, go outside and you can access the annex .There is more there." So I went out of the building, admiring the architecture and the grounds, and entered the other building. I said hi to the curator and she offered me a program to these works. I noted my sister-in-law's name on the program and was delighted that I had finally found it. However after looking at everything on the walls, I was dismayed to find that I had not yet discovered it. I went back to the curator's post. I waited patiently while some patrons were discussing a particular work in the museum. One said "How utterly unique that was!" Another said "How could anyone come up with that idea ?" A third was talking about the colors and the creativity. I listened carefully and heard the curator say that that was why the art work won first prize in that show. I then heard to my utter surprise that it was my sister-in- law's praise they were singing. They started pointing to the floor. That was where my sister-in-law's art work was displayed because it was a grid comprised of little pressed glass squares. Inside each square she had put the various dryer lint from each of many loads of clothes, and made a quilt like patchwork of the collected beautifully colored and textured and placed depressed lint pieces. What better present could I give my sister-in-law for her birthday which was the next day, than the live comments I heard about her artwork . This occurred all because every event I did that day at the exact time in the exact way led me to the exact moment when I arrived at that spot. I then remembered that at a psychic fair a couple of weeks earlier a psychic and I exchanged readings, and she told me I had a new spirit guide named Patrick. Well that explained the St Patrick's Day parade and all the synchronicity that happened after.

When I went to my mother's place one day I saw a dead bluejay on the patio. It looked like it had just fallen after it hit the window. It was vibrant and soft. I was thinking how different we humans are- stressing and full of haggling over this issue and that; the drama filled days of anger and jealousy and greed and dissatisfaction up until the last day. But this bird was undoubtedly flying and doing its tasks and enjoying the scenery of life and cooperating with its friends and family in its predirected ways of enjoying survival –doing what it always does ,enjoying the magnificence of the earth while performing its tasks to live, until the very second it died. Be like the bird, fly to the best of your ability and involvement until you die. I looked at a bird onetime as I was outside the retail store getting carriages and he had clearly smashed into the door falling to his death in seconds. I had gone outside once and then back out around two minutes later and suddenly saw the bird. What had happened in that instant right before he hit the door was that he probably had the philosophy that a customer earlier in the morning had which was that "You get what you get and you don't get upset." He probably did not agonize or cry. He lived his life to the fullest until the minute that he crashed into the door and that was it. Ah what lessons to be learned from a bird flying around until the second it did not. This reminds me of the major thought that I have to impart to you. Dead people morph in a minute. Way faster than humans. They morph with great difficulty if they morph at all. The living should take lessons from the dead.

When my third son broke his elbow he was about 14. We did the surgery route and several months later went back for a recheck. We asked if he could play sports again and the Dr. said of course. He said that the injured elbow was now indubitably stronger than the other one. Worry more about the one that had not been injured. That says to me that the broken parts can heal stronger than the original parts. Remember your broken heart may heal stronger than it was before. To morph remember that your broken parts often heal stronger than they were before.

Spirits come and tell me things often with pictures as well as words. I was in the relationship that I was finding so strenuously difficult to leave and they showed me a large circular stone wall. There was a semi-circular part behind me and as I looked to the front there was a 3 foot opening. They said if I stayed in the relationship, the wall would close up. I f I left the relationship, the hole would remain and lots of new experiences could happen for me in the big wide world outside the stone walls. With great difficulty I left. They also came to me a few months later.

They showed me a necklace. They said humans were like that. They could enslave or adorn you.

One day I rode an ambulance with my mother for one of her mini strokes. We were there together and she had awakened and my sister arrived into the room. She said to my 85 year old mother " Do you feel yourself ?" My mother said " Not really but, actually," she added, " I guess I do because this is who I am right now. " I said " Wow, you said that with Dad's wit" to which she immediately blurted out, "No I did't. It was my wit. I said it!" She was right. This is who I am right now is the huge working paradigm here. This is what the spirits and I are trying to convey .My mother was absolutely right.

I was talking to my second son who had just called to say hi. He was relating how well he had been doing for the second year in a row selling his wares, but had had an unusually slow time the last couple of weeks. He had not had any customers and it was a combination of the holidays and bad weather and who knows what else. We chatted about various things like life and girlfriends for about 20 minutes and then he said "There's a customer I'll call you back later." In five minutes he texted me and said, "This customer loves my name. She said to tell my Mom she's got good taste and obvious intellect."

My dog died. We put her down. My mate stayed inside and I went out. I was standing outside and the dog came to me. In real life she was Kelly. The voice came booming at me in a deep man's voice and she said in 6 weeks I would choose to have another dog. I really was not feeling that at that time and was surprised by the comment. Sure enough 6 weeks to the day my sister and my lover went up to a place near Boston to retrieve at dog that she had located but upon arrival there was no way I was about to receive a much misrepresented scrawny untrained not housebroken dog into my home. We went to a shelter my sister remembered was nearby and actually found a very loving new dog and brought him home. Kelly was right.

My mother's nurse was in the house and her car was parked in the driveway. I walked up and saw a picture attached to the dash. It was a woman but the name Richard was shown to me in front of it. I walked in and asked, "Maya, is that a picture of your dead mother in your car?" She said, "Yes." I said, "But I see the word Richard in front of the picture." She looked at me and exclaimed, "I have just come from my brother-in-law's funeral today. His name is Richard." I said, "Then he must be safely over there with your mother, his mother -in-law. "He's letting you know he's okay."

Three weeks ago I went to this café where I am trying to keep myself busy while I miss my ex lover. I try and I have met some nice people there. There is an extremely warm older artist there who goes with his sweet and intelligent wife. On this one occasion she asked me if I could tell her where she lost her keys, since I have alluded to the fact that I am a psychic and medium. She was pretty upset since she had lost them for a few days and they had not yet turned up. I asked her if she had backtracked and where had she gone when she noticed they were missing. She rattled off that she had shoveled leaves gone to the market, and to two drugstores. I told her I thought they were dropped in the parking lot of the second drug store, Ads, and that someone would find them and bring them to an authority within the building. She showed up for the next two weeks and still no keys. I insisted that was the information I was getting and that they'd turn up. The third week came and went. But the next day she called me at home and said "Thank you thank you. I just got a call from Ads. You were right. Somebody picked up my keys in the parking lot and they were mailed to the Ads headquarters and now they are sending them to me. I thought you'd like to know!" She is the sweetest 85 year old woman and I am happy to have helped.

Last week I had a plan to take my mother's car for a spin and fill it up on Saturday because that is one of my tasks in her household. I have this friend Cara who I talk with six times a week on the phone but rarely see because of our scheduling and life's different directions. This day I decided , "I'm going to call Cara and ask that she come for a ride with me while I am on this errand to recharge my mother's battery and get gas." I decided I could go across town and pick up some Chinese food at the restaurant where a couple of my friends work and surprise the crap out of them because I hate restaurants, while at the same time giving my mother an unusual treat for a change for dinner. I also had it in my head that I would go to a local discount store to get a mini pie for a quarter just to keep myself busy on a dateless Saturday night. I also do not like shopping and the last time I had been there was about 5 years earlier, but it was across the street from the restaurant.

When I arrived at my mother's house, I found to my dismay that the battery was already dead. This is a fairly common occurrence that we were trying to remedy since it is not driven too much and it was a nuisance to keep having to recharge it. I thought for a minute and said "Now my plans are screwed up and the restaurant is across town. I can not get my mother's car gas, and now I will once again just talk to Cara on the phone since I can not see her tonight." Well I decided to go anyway to change up my mother's dinner. I drove off and landed at the restaurant. I ordered there, saw my friends, and waited the amount of time it took to prepare the food. I paid for it and walked out. I said to myself, "What the heck I will go to the discount store while I am here anyway.". I walked in and there was Cara! In amazement I related the story and we marveled at how I had not been there in 5 years. I had not seen her in months, how big the store was and that she happened to be coming back to refill her coffee cup at the entrance. I had my visit with Cara after all.

One day I wanted to go to the resort town nearby by which houses a plantation as well as a waterfront shopping district. I always go to the plantation first and then the waterfront area to walk around and buy ice cream and cookies, but today I had the distinct urge to do the reverse. I arrived and put money in the meter and took lots of walks. which is my pattern. I bought a huge chocolate chip cookie which I would eat later at a shop where I sometimes put my cards. I walked over to the ma and pa store where I have developed a customer-boss relationship over the last several years that I have been going there. It is always fun to chit chat with her. I like to ask about her family and I always buy something and we both feel good. She has very affordable prices on very random interesting items. I picked up a pair of sandals for my son for five dollars and she said I could have a free gift because I made a purchase. Upon her questioning me if I wanted one of her little blank boxes with a surprise inside I said " Sure." I put it in my pocket and told her I would open it someday when I really needed a little treat.

I continued on my little day and went back to the meter and saw that it had plenty of time. The meter maids love to give out their tickets so I always check. The spirits told me to put more money in. I looked at the meter again. I checked the time. I saw how ridiculous or so I thought it was, but by now I listen to the spirits and put some more money in the meter. I was going to eat the popcorn I had brought to nibble on the way to the plantation, but they came back and said I had to stand in front of my car and eat the popcorn. Now I am not the type of person to stay still, but I obeyed. I was munching on my popcorn for a good twenty minutes but my feet would not move. I was eyeballing the meter and the shoreline and the bag of popcorn. It was delicious but I was wondering what I was doing standing there. Then I looked in front of me and saw one man sitting in a car listening to a ball game. He was older and sort of dozing. I figured he was waiting for a shopping spouse. I looked at the car beside his and noticed an enraged looking man who was leaning on his car and alternately pacing. I started to think he too was pissed at having to wait for his wife shopping.

At that second he darted over to me. He said "Why are you here?" I breathed in a breath and the reading began. I tuned in to him and looked at him. I said "You are an alcoholic and you feel disconnected from everyone and everything in life." He stared at me and cried. I said, "This is why I am here." He said, "You're right. I am an alcoholic. And I don't feel connected to anyone. I want to die." I said, "You can not do that. It is harder than you find this life and your issues now, if you do that." "Are you sure?" he said. "Yes I am positive." I said. I start to see the name Mike, who by now I knew was this guy's dead father. I start to say that "No matter what you have done or did not do it is not your time to go. You can still fix things." I said "I have a man here and he says he is Mike. I am a psychic and I see things."

The man said that he was his father and that he wanted him to go there too. I said, "No that it wasn't his time." I told him that it was too bad that he did not feel loved by his parents that he was fed table scraps as a kid, but that he should look at all the people passing by in front of us. He looked. I told him that he had as much a right to be loved as they did. He was no better or worse than any man woman or child walking on that block. He kept crying and then looked up and started poking me. This would usually bother me because people have tried to steal my energy that way but this felt different. I watched him then I asked, "Why are you poking me?" After he kept poking me for awhile I repeated, "Why are you doing this?" He answered, "Because you must be an angel. I am poking you to see what you feel like. Are you?" "I guess kind of. I function at a higher vibration. And I know why I was here. It was for you right now so we could have this little talk." I said "Turn around." He said "No". I repeated the request for him to turn and he stubbornly said "No." I had in my thoughts that I was going to show him the beautiful ocean. He had other thoughts in mind and he said, "I will not turn around because if I do you will be gone." I said, "It is true I do have to go soon. But let's turn together .",as I let him grab my arm to turn with me.

I showed him the ocean and told him that he was made up of the same stuff as the ocean and that he was as worthy of being loved as anyone and that he should stand in front of a mirror everyday and give himself a hug until he knew he was worthy of it and then others would start to hug him. I said I had to go now.

I left to go to the bathroom, chuckling at how I had to refill my meter knowing I wanted to be at the plantation by 2:30pm. It was now 3:00pm.I walked away knowing I had just loved a total stranger and had eaten my popcorn at the car for quite an interesting rich reason. I returned to the car to head to the plantation. On a second thought, I opened the door and reached in to get the prize cookie. I walked over to the man in the car and tapped on the window. He tried to grab me up into the car, but I said "Here, this cookie I got this morning, but you can have my cookie." I handed it to him, he stared at it and I left.

I headed to the plantation and thinking the whole time that I would go to the plantation show at the auditorium today. When I took the kids over the years we must have seen it over 40 times. So in the past years of my visiting the place I just skipped it. Today after passing the membership desk, I headed for the auditorium to see the show for old times or new times. To my utter surprise I looked around and oddly saw a liquor bar and popcorn machine. It was so odd to see that at this children's plantation. "That is strange, there must be something special going on today", I was thinking. As I was about to find the curator I rested my eyes on a sign that read "Special program today 2-4pm on Lesbians in Pilgrim days." I was shocked. The lady outside the auditorium came running over and said "This presentation started at 2:30pm. Please go right in as it is in progress. It is fine." I was shocked to see about 80 gay men sitting listening and the rest scattered lesbians in the auditorium smiling and hanging on every word the slender butch type lady in front was speaking. Since I arrived late due to my earlier psychic experience, the symposium ended.

I rushed to the front where she said she would take a few questions and I waited patiently while a few men, who were in witches' garb, were asking gently about gay witches at that time. That was also fascinating because I met my first witch as defined by her earlier that week. The conversation ended and it was my turn. I identified my self as a newly out lesbian and in fact I had just told my daughter a few weeks before. Suddenly the museum special events coordinator told the presenter she had to clean up to get the stage ready for the next presenter. I waited and then walked to the back and asked if I could at least have her card so maybe I could contact her and ask her things I had clearly missed. She said, "Of course," handing me her card. I stared at it in disbelief. It was my daughter's address, the same college my daughter attends several states away. I said, "This is really your address? You must be a professor at my daughter's school. Do you know her?" I told her a few things about my daughter. She said she had just talked to her yesterday. I said, "Leave this between you and me," and I walked away baffled. A typical day in my life.

A couple of weeks later when I went to go outside I grabbed the very shirt I was wearing the day this all happened. In the pocket something was protruding a little. I reached in and there was the tiny box the shopkeeper/boss had given me as a bonus that day. I remembered I wanted to go on my walk to get a magnet for my fridge where I post things, so as I headed out I opened the box. Inside was a little magnet with a picture of a clipper ship on it. Not only that, the amazing part was that it was a replica of the only picture I have that Adam drew 15 years earlier of a clipper ship with sails just like that. It was Adam saying hi and I got a magnet I had been shopping for for a while but could not seem to find.

One day I was sitting in my house on a Saturday afternoon at 1:30pm. Suddenly I said I had to go to my mother's house and talk to the nurse Cara. It was totally oddball that I had to go then, because I always go in the evenings. I even had a couple of children home and told them I had to go, I would be back. They were a bit surprised but would stay together having lunch until I got back. When I arrived at my mother's Cara was telling me that she had a belly ache, but went along to get my mother dressed. While my mother was in the restroom Cara sat on the couch and said she would call her son at the end of her shift and get him to bring her to the emergency room. I asked if she was really all right, and she said she could wait. It was just an unusually intense belly ache. I was not sure that she could wait and I asked her if I could make my mother's food instead of her . She agreed and then went to the bathroom to get my mother. I came in to the living room and set up my mother's table and turned and saw Cara on the floor doubled over in pain. I asked her if I should call an ambulance by calling 911 and she said " Yes." Within 15 minutes of my being there, Cara was sent off in the ambulance and I stayed to watch my mother. P.S. Cara's colon had lesions and she stayed in the hospital for two weeks, medicine being poured into her by I.V. to detoxify her system. I visited her there and at her home after. She is fine now, has been back working and we are friends.

Whenever my 25 year old son lives with me, unbeknownst to him, I can sense when he comes home. Over a period of at least eight years, whenever he comes home in the night, whenever his car is at the top of the street about 18 houses away I wake up and when he pulls into the driveway I giggle.

One day I went into the store and had $10.00 in my pocket. I noticed there was soda on sale and also oatmeal. I brought the random cans and oatmeal to the register and showed the girl a $10 bill. I said that this is what I have on me. She rang it up and said "It is exactly $10." I smiled as I handed her my exact $10 dollar bill thinking how psychic that was.

I find psychic things happening while working at the store. For instance, when I was walking by the register, I turned and saw a customer walking out with a big box. I turned to her and I said "Oh, you have a lot of books in that box." And she looked at me baffled and smiled. She said "Not yet, but right this minute I am on my way to pick them up. They are waiting for me and I am going to put them in these gift boxes I just purchased." I said, "I am psychic and that is why I saw the books." She said, "I guess you are." And we both smiled as she walked out of the store.

In another observation, I was reminded how nature teaches us things. Sam, my dog was found to have a bullet in him somewhat after I brought him home from the shelter. It had escaped their notice; he was walking on three legs sometimes. He was still happy even so. One day last week he howled in pain as his hurt leg had seemed to cramp. He howled as it maneuvered itself into a different and painful position. The next day after the pain, he walked on all four legs. Pain precedes proper functioning or advanced functioning sometimes. There are some things in life you cannot change.

There are natural things like weather., and unnatural things like metaphoric or real bullets in life. You can plan preventions with your brain -like build teepees strong enough for the wind or walking your dog in a private area to defecate and not on a child's area to play .An unpredicted storm may come or wind too strong to stand up against. A dog may have the runs before you get to a designated area. You do your best to prepare and protect, but the environment, circumstance or experience may have other plans. Walk away from powerful negative situations and people you cannot change- immediate problems can occur. To continue the dog story this is what happened.

. I had to have my dog go through some surgery to remove the bullet in his leg which upon investigation we had discovered from his pound days. It had begun to cause him too much pain, and he was only using three legs on a constant basis. After this procedure he was recovering remarkably well and I was proceeding with our usual walking routine. As I was walking back from the store marveling at Sam's four legged capabilities and how much better he was doing, a lady stopped me and yelled, "Hey do you know your dog is limping! Do you know something is wrong with him?" Perspective is different. She did not have information I had to confirm his ultimate well-being and his actual state of progression to being better. Information, therefore leads to accuracy, but information is not equal. People come from or live from only their own perspective, even if they care.

I was walking down the street to the post office and I saw a neighbor in the car with her window up, but I still got a message. I knocked at the window at the intersection, and asked if she wanted to hear a message. She knows I do this stuff. She nodded and I told her that her friend Cheryl wanted to say hi. She immediately cried and said that that was a stewardess with whom she had worked for many years who had just passed. She was quite relieved to know she was all right. The power of being able to be used by spirit and the other helpers and the people desperately trying to communicate is an utmost rewarding and deeply wonderful experience.

Often I will have silly things happen, like I will suddenly say "Oh I need toilet paper" and "I have to go to one of the two drug stores on the strip near my house." I will walk in and sure enough there will be a buy one get one free special that day. Or as it happened the other day, I am in between physicians because a challenged a physician's comment and I wanted a second opinion. So I was wondering where I am going to get my flu shot, and a drug store that was near me announced that they were not going to have it at this location this year. I just did not know what to do .I thought that maybe my thyroid doctor will give them or my gynecologist. I was not really sure and it was pressing on me. A couple days after that I got an intuition they said "You've got to go to "Ashley's." I said to myself I have not been there for fifteen years .It is a little bit across town and I did not know if I should just go check it out, but I honor the spirits , soI did go to check it out and see what bargains they have. I walked in and sure enough there was a big sign in the lobby that said "Flu shots given daily 10-4". I thought I was just going to see the bargains but the spirits knew more.

When I approached a stable one time, on the way into the corral I saw a horse lying down and I said "Oh" and somebody whispered "Oh that horse was struck by a car." They said I could take my ride and I was still compelled to go riding. While they were tending to this horse I was in the corral riding. All of a sudden I flipped into being an Indian, I felt like I was an Indian riding a horse. The Indian started telling me things .What he said was "There's a horse named Coconut in this corral somewhere" and he kept saying "Bill, Bill is going to be okay." So I finished riding, they did what they did with that unfortunate horse and when I got off and dismounted I asked the stable hand if he knew anyone named Bill around here? And he said "Well yes, he owns that horse that just got hit by that car, but he will be okay because he also owns a horse named Coconut who is doing very well in the stall over there fourth one on the left." I said "Oh, okay cool."

Interestingly enough while I was waiting for the operation on my thyroid aforementioned, I was in the pre anesthesia operation room and suddenly my levels escalated .I could feel the spirits come to protect me and make me feel better and lighter .Then an attendant came over and asked "What do you do for a living?" and for the first time ever I said "I'm a psychic." She was very excited and I said "Yes well I can see things." and she said "Yeah, like what?" and I said "Well I can see that you have a scar on your elbow and I see a broken bike." She freaked and said "I fell off my bike a long long time ago and I still have the scar and she rolled up her sleeve to show me. She then went and told somebody else and while was sitting there lying waiting wondering what is going on I hear a man yell over from another patients bedside "Yes well I bet she can't tell me anything! "I said "Yes I can, you became a grandparent this week" and he said "Oh yes well what day?" and I said "on the 26th". He grew silent, then another one came and they started coming, I did about five readings while I was waiting for the operation to begin. I told another woman that she was very upset because she wanted to have another child and she only had one and I said to love the one. I said the only way she could possibly get pregnant is through lots of scientific procedures like in vitro and she just looked at me and said that is how she got this one. I told her to love that one, don't worry about what is going to happen later on. Then another woman came over and said she had 8 miscarriages and asked did I ever see her having a child. I said "I do see you adopting a boy in two years, after that you're going to have a biological boy and biological girl." Later on I bumped into her and she had adopted a boy, had a biological boy and a biological girl starting two years after that.

A cousin of mine who was dying had nurses taking care of her. I visited her periodically and they called me near the end and asked me how long this cousin was going to live. I said that I see the number 2 but I don't know if its two weeks or two months but I see two. As it happens she did die 2 months later. The week before she passed away one of the nurses called me to tell me I should come over because she thought she might be passing away that night. I went over and I walked into my cousin Terry's room and I suddenly walked back out and told the nurse that I sensed two spirits were about to receive her on the other side. One was Fred, that was her brother, and one was Diane, that was her sister. The nurse said that that was really weird. "Why would they come to take her to the other side? She never really talked about them. She talked about her other brother and sisters." I was chit chatting with the nurse when I was telling her this when all of a sudden Terry shouted in a loud voice "Fred! Fred!" and I said "Do you see Fred?" and she said "Yes" and then she said "Who is that woman in the corner?" and I said "What's she look like" and she said "Well I don't know what she looks like exactly, but who is she? She's right there!" and I said "Diane" I went back out and the nurse freaked. Terry died the following week .Before the funeral I went for a walk to the variety store. . There are always these two men at the variety store in the morning and they sit and read the news paper and chit-chat between themselves and discuss the lottery number. We tease each other because we all play the lottery a little bit. This time one of the men shouted out loud "Terry Smith died!" and I looked at him and I walked over to him and I said "Why did you shout her name out?" and he looked at me and said "I have no idea. I'm reading the obituaries and I just did!" I looked at him and grinned and knew that she had given me a sign that she was okay. I went to the funeral and told Terry's nurse and we knew that Terry was okay.

My sister was going to the hospital to have some mildly complicated surgery. My own grandparents and great grandparents do not often come in, but today one of my grandfathers made a bold entrance. While my brother was driving her to the hospital, my grandfather said "Call her." I had no idea what he was going to say, until she picked up the phone. He then said to my sister and I repeated verbatim " 'This is grandpa and I will be with you today; particularly in the operating room. You will know this by the name tag some attendant will be wearing with my name'." Sure enough, she called me when she got there, and told me there was this huge good looking man taking her name and information and when she looked down at his badge, she was startled when she saw my grandfather's name. Also, she was in surgery way longer than expected due to an unexpected problem. She came out fine and undoubtedly more of a believer. But she is my sister so she'll forever tease me and maybe not tell.

OTHER READINGS

I HAVE BEEN ASKED IF I AM AN ANGEL.
I KNOW I FUNCTION AT A HIGHER
VIBRATION AND THAT IS WHY I CAN
DO THE READINGS. THEY FUNCTION
AND LIVE IN THEIR WAY AT A HIGHER
VIBRATION. BUT I KNOW I AM NOT
AN ANGEL BECAUSE SOMETIMES MY
HEART HURTS AND I DO NOT THINK
AN ANGEL'S HEART WOULD EVER
HURT. ERGO I CA N NOT BE AN ANGEL
(YET).

THERE IS THIS VEIL I LOOK THROUGH.
I AM A VISUAL PERCEIVER OF
SPIRITS MOSTLY. IT IS A TELEPATHIC
COMMUNICATION; THE SPIRITS DO
NOT MOVE THEIR LIPS.

These spirits tell me things by sort of silent thinking.
I get words flashing across my vision. Letters that form
words or sayings come. Sometimes whole sentences form
as well. The dead like to communicate that they are okay.
It does not matter that they have been dead for a day
or eighty years, they still love to come through. Maybe
someday you can see like I do .I would suggest that you
believe. It might happen sooner than you think.

Often times grandparents come through, parents,
nephews, children who have passed. My job, I feel, is to
bring light. I am doing this to show that there is life after

death. If a voice is particularly distinct or maybe raspy I will hear it, and on occasion I get a certain smell if it is a particular connection. Sometimes they come in and say a silly thing like "You at a banana today" or they might identify themselves by name. I would say I get names in 99% of my readings of either the spirits or the listeners or people in the listeners current lives and the discussion of events that are going on.

Readings can sort of be categorized into feel good readings or readings where the spirits impart specific information or tools for the hopeful listener.

Here are examples of phone readings:

I do phone readings as well. One reading stands out. She was in Florida and was referred to me by a cousin who I had done a reading for. I told her the name of her dead mother Dot. Dot was describing a white sweater the woman was wearing and I told her that she was sitting on a patio in a white chair, which she affirmed. The mother continued that the woman was drinking coffee out of an odd shaped mug. It was off white and had some coloration but it had kind of like ears. She laughed and was completely scared and said "I'm drinking coffee from a Mickey Mouse mug as we speak." She was delighted that her mother had come through. I did another phone reading with somebody in New York, and her mother had passed. I told her that her mother was here and I named her Jenny. Jenny wanted to say hi to other siblings and said, "I want to say hi to Carol and Joanne." There were three sisters and she was thrilled that I had named her mother as well as her two sisters. Then the mother said there was an occasion coming up and she will attend. Then I said I suddenly see a young boy and I got a letter J. He's trying on ties and getting dressed up, he has a jacket and pants to match. He's standing in front of the mirror trying to get it all together, not quite right yet. Then she said, "There is an occasion- do you know it?" And I said, "I'm getting there's a Bar Mitzvah and she said "Yes there is!" And as we speak she said her son was trying on his older brother's suit that he wore for his Bar Mitzvah and it needed to be tailored and his name was Jethro.

There was another occasion when something interesting happened. A woman had called me from New Jersey and said she lost her dog and did I have any way of knowing where he was? His name was Malcolm and I intuited what I thought and I told her that I really thought this dog was inside somewhere and he was safe." He's not outside, he's inside somewhere. He'll be okay, there is a roof over his head and he'll be home in the morning." There was extra concern because it had started to rain hard.

We hung up and I turned the TV on and there was a conversation some teacher in a school was having and the teacher said "Malcolm's here in class today, so glad he's back." I called the girl up and I told her and I said "I really think your dog is going to be okay after I saw this." The next morning she called me at 7 in the morning to tell me that he was locked in a barn accidentally, and he did have a roof over his head. They discovered him, and he was safe and sound.

Here are some examples of feel good readings:

What makes a reading a reading is not imagination or wishing or guessing ,as I have said. I told this to a woman who came to me so distraught. I did not of course know her or what the problem was in any way, until I named her dead husband Tommy in two seconds. Everybody goes fishing, but in this reading I saw him fishing with a unique set of fishing gear. He was not in a boat. His pants were rolled up walking into a stream. There were rocks all along it, and what was distinctive about his fishing pole was that it was handmade. The scene was occurring maybe a year ago but the pole was made out of a long piece of branch or wood and a string tied to it. She howled with certain laughter and said "That is what he did." He also said that it was Valentine's Day soon and were he here he would buy her caramel chocolates and yellow roses. To her utter shock she called me two weeks later with the report that her fellow office worker amazingly enough decided to buy her some caramel chocolates for Valentine's Day. Her next door neighbor in her apartment for the first time ever handed her some yellow roses. This offers hope that there is another dimension. You do not necessarily see it, but it is there. It has the potential to take away your pain for even a second.

A woman was referred to me who was a total skeptic but was hurting so badly that she gave me the call. She changed her appointment a few times but did show on the third try. I told her I saw the name James in the first second. She said that was her dead husband's name. He told me he was okay and sent his regards to his daughter Nancy and his son Tom. She was happy and went home and called me the next day to report that she played his grave number and won the few thousand dollars that night.

A lady came to me totally distraught about losing her father. She needed to know if he was okay. He had been her best friend. I did not know why I was saying this, but I said what I felt. I turned to her and said "When people die, they are perfectly fine. Their ailments go away. For instance, if you have your legs amputated when you are here, then when you cross over you suddenly have your legs and are whole again." She glared at me and her jaw dropped. She said " Right before my father had died he had one leg amputated from the hip and then the other leg amputated from the knee." We were both pretty shocked and delighted that he was clearly letting us know that he was okay. She felt she could go on with a little more peace knowing what she now knew about him.

I did a reading for a guy once and he was extremely distraught about his mother who had passed. He was hopeful that he could connect. He stood there and I had a vision of a birthday cake and the name Amy. He cried that today was her birthday and her name was Amy. She continued "Say hi to Chris". "That is my sister" he said staring amazedly. The mother continued, " 'She gardens with the precision of a Doctor'". The young man again amazed, managed to tell me as we were speaking "My sister is home right now gardening and she is a Doctor." He was tearfully thrilled to have made the connection with his mother through the reading and somewhat relieved, felt better and went home.

One of the first readings I ever did was for a girl at work with whom I had no particular relationship. She worked upstairs and I down. One day she was wildly complaining about how much her toe hurt. She had told other people about how the Doctor couldn't make it better and it was so purple and sore. She crossed in front of me going up the stairs and I sheepishly told her I do this healing thing and I would not even have to touch her and would she like some. She said "Okay". She turned around and came back down the stairs. I told her to sit down which she did on a pile of boxes in the stockroom. I put my hands above her sneaker, still on her foot, and gave her Reiki. As I was doing this she started smiling saying "What are you doing exactly? It feels better." I told her it was energy and she would feel better for sure. She started saying " I can move it, it feels so much better". As we were sitting there I saw a grandmother materialize to the right of her. I said "Do you believe in the afterlife?" She said "I don't know." I said I saw a spirit who wanted to be acknowledged and did she want me to keep going with my conversation with the spirit and her. She said very hesitantly, "Okay." The spirit insisted on telling me to tell the girl to plant the lilac tree. I have learned not to filter messages in any way. The girl started to cry. Apparently she and her husband had been fighting about this lilac tree. "We have discussed this angrily for two weeks because we are moving and I want to transfer the lilac tree that I had planted in honor of my deceased grandmother but it died. He says don't bring it and I am persisting." She recognized the grandmother by her clothes and features from my description. She ended up digging up that tree, bringing it to the new location and it bloomed.

It was the anniversary of the death of the woman's mother, when the woman, very sad and miserable came to me. The mother came through with a story about strawberry pie. The woman started smiling. The spirit talked about how they went strawberry picking and it was a time when lots of relatives were coming for a weekend. The woman started actually laughing about how many strawberry pies were actually made and consumed that weekend and told how it was a big family joke. The spirit clearly wanted to come through with some story that would take the weight off the sadness her daughter still felt.

A lady called me up because it was the anniversary of her first husband's death. She had dreamt about him that night and wanted to touch base if she possibly could. I told her I saw a beautiful man with blonde hair. She affirmed his physical features. I continued "I see a guitar." She said he played the guitar and as a matter of fact she had a degree in music and they sang together. She was immediately feeling better, but then asked me a specific question which always makes me breathe a little harder. She said in the 70's he gave her a plant which has continued to bloom all these years up to 2009 and did I know the type? We live in the north and this was somewhat unfamiliar and a surprise, but I asked and he gave me the response, so I said "Cactus is what I see." She shrieked and cried "You are right – that is what it is! .He really is okay."

I was doing a reading for someone and was certain that her deceased grandfather was trying to make contact with her stepfather who was here. The spirits were informing me that this person had not seen her stepfather in a while and wanted to. She acknowledged the truth in that statement and said she had not seen him in 7 years, and did not know quite how to initiate contact after a family separation issue, ending in a kind of rift. The reading was over and she was going to her car to get money and suddenly shrieked, "Susan! That is my stepfather's car pulling in to park over there!" I said, "You are sure?" "Yes!" she said. She walked over and they started talking. I drove away smiling at the wonder of things in the universe.

An acquaintance of mine's father died and I was going to pay respect, because I felt that I should even though I did not know her family well in any way. On the way I kept getting the name "Bill, Bill, Bill" and when I arrived I got in the line and heard people talking quietly. When I got up to the family my friend said "Hi, this is Bill Jr. he's a spitting image of my father Bill Sr." Clearly that was the spirit of Bill letting us know he was okay on the other side.

When I read people, most of the time, I walk. And I was walking in this chilly air, in November, around the block. It was dark and the sky was gray, it seemed to smell like winter. All of a sudden I smelled apple- cranberry pie. It was a wonderful pure smell and I looked at the person and I said "I have a spirit here who is presenting us with apple-cranberry pie," and she says " 'It's only made with cinnamon and sugar, but the important part is that I soaked the apple pieces with the skin still on first in water and cinnamon that was my own touch'." And she looked at me and said yes that was her grandmother's recipe and only she the only granddaughter knows how to do it now." That was the family secret.

I did a reading for a woman and I told her that her father named Steve had come through and he was with his wife, on the other side. They were talking about this woman's weight being too low. She said yes since they both died which had been fairly recent, she had lost her appetite. They described a restaurant they went to with big windows and he said that if he were going to order food there it would be chowder. The woman was quite delighted because he considered himself the king of chowder making, and that was an affirmation that we were talking to him. He also said that he was hovering around his apartment quite often and he wasn't going to leave until the organ was gone. The woman laughed and laughed and said yes she had packed up lots of things and pretty much everything was out of the apartment except his organ. Her mother said "You know you really should eat some pie." She said that was her mother's favorite thing to bake, her signature was her pies. She did feel better. Also I told her there needs to be some communication with your cousin Paul. She said "Well that's crazy because Paul lives in Australia and I haven't really communicated with him in many years, several years, it would be odd" and I said well spirits now keep telling me that there's going to be a phone call from Paul or to Paul, around Paul. At the end of the reading she got home and called me and said "Paul called; he's getting married and wanted to invite me to the wedding." Also, just before she left I said do you know a girl named Ann? And your parents are pretty happy that you have a friend, she's got to be a very close friend, because they're always happy when you have someone to share love with and good times with and get support from. She said "yes, but I haven't seen her in a little while, but I really do have a close relationship with Ann." No sooner had she gotten in her car, starting to drive away when this woman ran over to the car. The woman I had read yelled out the window "this is Ann." Very cool, truth from the spirits.

I was doing a reading last week, and we were walking along and I was telling this girl how she really needed to try to get her boyfriend to clean the house. She should threaten him by putting the dirty pizza boxes and dirty underwear and old things he left around the house on the front seat of his car if he did not clean up. Then she giggled and giggled and said she just threatened him with that. Then I kept saying "roof roof" like I was barking. It was clear that I was connecting with her father, and he was showing me a dog which was obviously on this side. She laughed and said "Well my dog is Rufus" and her father on the other side smiled and continued . He kept emphasizing that he wanted to acknowledge Victoria. She was the step mother (so the young girl then verbalized) on this side. Her father said on a serious note that it was okay that after three solid years, she had just dispersed his ashes. She acknowledged that there had been a three year battle about who would get the ashes. She, her mom and her father's mom all had strong feelings for receiving the ashes. She and her mother had finally allowed her dad's mother to have the ashes. He said " 'That's fine, my energy is not only in those ashes. Go home and put on the necklace you have with the silver heart shaped pendant on it, in which there is a picture of me'". She smiled and cried, remembering how she saved the necklace in her top drawer. She said she would go home and put the necklace on. She hugged me and felt better.

One day I was doing a house reading and her husband was deceased and he came through by name and he said "I'm Jim and I'm here and my wife should do more art work." She showed me a picture on the wall that she had done years earlier and it was stunning. He said he really would like to say hi to his friends Jack and Peter. Suddenly he was pressuring me to look at some photos in the photo albums that were lying closed on the refrigerator. I said emphatically, we really need to get those photo albums down and look at them and she looked at me and said, "Okay." Then we took them down and opened the first page and there were snapshots of Jack and Peter.

One day, I went to the post office and there was a lady in front of me who said she had my card for about 4 years, however she was nervous and had not contacted me yet. She said "I am still thinking about it." Two days later, I went to the drug store and crossed in front of her car in the parking lot. She stopped me and said " I guess I am ready for the reading soon" and proceeded to make an appointment for two days later. When we met, her father came through and said "You have two daughters- one chubby and one thin". She said "Yes." I told her that he particularly misses the chubby one and spelled her name out as M-A-I-A. She was very surprised at the correct spelling of the name because she intentionally spelled it in a non traditional way. She was excited and affirmed that we had contacted her father.

I did a reading and the woman Diane started walking beside me. I took three steps and told her I had someone named Ken here. She cried, "That's the name of my dead husband. He died three months ago. That is why I wanted to see you." I told her there was a big letter 'B" in front of me. "My son's name is Burt." Just at that moment her phone started ringing. I continued quickly while she looked at the dialer, "The spirits say that you are thinking of moving." She said, "Yes I am and I just talked in the last three days about moving away and trading houses with Burt." She looked at her continually ringing phone and it was Burt.

Here are some examples of some specific tools and information that is offered:

I did a reading for a young woman and her dead Aunt Mary came through and told me that this girl was really stuck. The frustration and anger that she felt about her divorcing husband was incessant and consuming. I suggested to her that even though she was living (free of charge too) with her mother, she was missing all the love her mother was sending her way in every conversation. She was feeling that nobody loved her, and yet in every conversation with her mother she was merely whining about how her ex would not change and step up to the plate of his responsibility. That is okay to a point, but then all the love of her mother was rolling off, and the woman could not feel any.

I did a reading for a woman whose great Aunt Carol came through to discuss how this lady's marriage was going. Every day this woman was reacting by adjusting to how her husband happened to come in every day. If he was happy that behavior followed, if he was severing and alienated that disconnective behavior was manifested. This girl did not have a plan. She had lost herself in this situation. She did not know if her marriage was existent or not, but instead of confronting the situation and her needs, she merely reacted to his demanding nature. Nobody won. The Aunt insisted that the woman get in touch again with who she was and have a plan for getting what she wanted in life as well as out of the marriage and be herself and see if the game would change between them. Nothing was going to change unless she reframed this experience as one in which she had to learn and morph. Five years from now everything would be the same if the situation of only being a pile of reactions versus having a plan were still the mindset. To morph then, realize that you are supposed to be getting something out of this challenge if you are feeling uncomfortable.

A reading can morph you in a minute. An example of this is the woman who came to me on tons of meds and also had quit her job because she was so off her center. I told her that I immediately see an Aunt Dawn. She acknowledged her deceased Aunt. The Aunt said " 'She had an abortion. She feels impure and loss and never got over it. It was 10 years ago. She also has three other children, but it is not enough'". I repeated the message and the girl cried and said that was the complete truth. I told her that the spirits continued with their advice which was to get involved in a school program or something else to put the love she would have given to that child toward others. I saw her taking care of other children who were not hers biologically in her home as well in some way. Three months later she came back. She was off her meds had taken in three foster children and got a new job better suited to her evolving self.

In a reading, a young man had come just to try it out. He was in his twenties, not particularly noticeably attractive. But I picked up that he was a supremely gentle, industrious, loyal sweet guy, but again clearly not what you would call a stud. I noted "Your dead Uncle Tony is here and says you are about to purchase a gas station. Your investment will be about $ 25,000 at the gate." The boy acknowledged that that was right. I continued, "There is going to be a girl that you are going to meet in about four months at a holiday gathering of some sort." He said "Yeah right. That is about to happen. I have not dated much in my life at all." I persisted and said, "She's going to be very short with shoulder length sandy hair and you're really going to have a good time with her." That was the reading. About 5 months later, I bumped into him. He had a happy but amazed look on his face. He said he had gone to a Thanksgiving function and saw a girl across the room who fit my description exactly. He had the courage to go talk to her, and they were happily dating. He was engaged several months later and he bought the gas station too.

There was a young couple in their twenties and they wanted to move to Boston, but neither one yet had a job. They were kind of of the mindset that once they moved there things would materialize, as they had been desperately searching the job network. They located an apartment and were about to lock into a $1000 a month lease, when the young man suddenly decided it wasn't appropriate to move until at least one of them had a job. The pillow of money they had would easily possibly have been depleted if their plans did not materialize. He was suddenly offered a job in a toy warehouse factory. While he was considering this first offer, several other job offers presented. He was finally offered the job he was waiting for and decided to accept. When he called to refuse the job at the toy warehouse, the manager told him that it was a position for a male or female. The man's girlfriend was then able to take that position and they both had solid work. I was reading the young woman and she was desperately trying to get a job in the engineering field. I kept tripping over the letters of a company I saw she would be applying to. I kept saying, "I see C-A-D". She said that there was a company that she was applying to that had the letters C-A-T and other letters, but I could not seem to say the name of the company. She got back to me after the reading a few weeks later, and said that she was hired to do special work in the architectural firm, because her specialty was an ability to use a program called C-A-D.

I did a reading for a young man one time. "Jim" his father immediately appeared. Upon hearing this name, the handsome seemingly composed young man started to cry. I continued, "He says hi to your half brother Chris and your half sister Nancy." The boy acknowledged these correct names. "He says he is sorry for the completely different upbringings of the two sets of children. He realized that he was in attendance at all the half brother's baseball games whereas he wasn't much of a father to you, and never attended any of your games. He said if it's any consolation, he attends every one of your son's soccer games." The young man acknowledged that his son does play soccer. The spirit continued and I repeated " ' I was so young when I had you'." His appearance was like a cool biker type guy in a black leather jacket smoking a cigarette leaning against a garage. I related this and the young man said he was a garage mechanic and that was his style. He continued, " 'You'll understand everything when you cross over I mean why things were the way they were, but for now just understand that none of it was your fault and I love you and I will always have your back. I'm your angel now and I'll be with you forever. And by the way thanks for liking my toy airplane collection. I'm glad you have it and appreciate it'." The young man looked at me and said "I know he's really here, I have his toy airplane collection. They're like little matchbox type cars. I feel like I am in a hot air balloon ride right now. For the first time in my life I feel better. I've carried this negative feeling about my father forever. You lifted me up. Thank you so much." He hugged me and left.

This woman sat down. I did not know her. I had never spoken a word to her. I said "I have Mary here, she appears to be on your mother's side. She is in spirit and I think she's your grandmother." The woman agreed she had a dead grandmother named Mary there. The grandmother continued " 'I have Chris here'." The woman cried that that was her brother's name. The grandmother said that " 'Chris is okay and he was with her'." The woman could barely say aloud that he had just been killed and she was so happy to know he was safely with the grandmother. I continued to relate what the grandmother was saying. " 'We want to acknowledge Richard and Mark and Donna'." "Those are our other siblings" she said. I suddenly saw another name as well as a rope around a male's neck. I said "There is a Jay and there is a lasso type rope hung around his neck." She blurted out, "You are really in clear contact ! My brother Jay hung himself not long ago!" I continued with silly stuff like, "Your father George says you had some apple pie yesterday. He says it's okay to have a sweet slice of life. You need a little good and sweetness." She was shocked at everything and said she had absolutely had the piece of pie yesterday and that exact flavor. It was totally out of character. That is a typical reading.

Another woman sat down and did not tell me her name. She did not ask anything or say anything about why she was there. I looked at her " I'm getting the name Don something." She said, "My name is Donna." I said,

"Your mother is here calling you and delighted you came. She says hello to your brother Rick." The woman agreed she had a brother Rick. She was quite surprised, but was completely overtaken when I continued. "Your mother says you are stubborn about your diet and that you need to eat sugarless cookies and stop taking all the donuts." The lady laughed and said she was diagnosed with diabetes and was supposed to watch her diet. The mother said she was completely going astray and refused to give up her sweet snacks. I then came forth with a big comment from the mother " 'I never kissed you enough and was not the mother you wanted me to be'." The woman started sobbing. "She is grabbing up your cheek and saying ' I love you I love you, I love you and will always be with you'." The spirit grabbed up the lady's cheek and kissed and kissed it. " 'I am sorry. I apologize for not telling you I love you in a way you could see it. But please know I always did.'" The woman stared at me. She said for the first time in her seventy odd years she was going to go to bed with sweet thoughts of her mother. She had waited all her life for an apology from her mother in life and never got it. Now she had one from the other side. It was feeling pretty good even then.

A dead spirit came through by the name of David and said that he was offering the niece a pile of pancakes. She said that pancakes were his Sunday morning specialty. The spirit said this was a metaphor. She was going through some difficult, seemingly awful times. And he said " 'Life is like pancakes. You flip them over. If your life is one way it flips fast. If you're happy one day you will be sad or frustrated or blue but it flips fast. You will soon be happy and life will be fruitful and it flips soon again. It is also round. This particularly symbolizes the spin of life, the round and round and round again in the cycle'." She felt better from the wisdom.

I did a reading where the dead spirits came through by the name of John and Deana and they said they were watching their son become the alcoholic they had been. They also mentioned the name of his best friend Mike who was also an alcoholic. I was reading the wife. The spirits said, " 'Give him a slip of paper which will look like a coupon, and tell him he now has permission by this ticket to feel the pain of his neglect- filled childhood. Because if he only uses will power to stop his drinking for a time or two, he will go back if he doesn't start to feel his pain and work through it and the whys of his drinking habits'." I was reading his wife, who has the obligation to offer help but leave him if in the fifteenth year of his drinking he does not stop, to leave so as to save her daughters and herself from further abusive non-growing existences, so they informed me.

A clerk was in the back room at my workplace, unbeknownst to me. While she was there she felt something touching her back and she knew all the people were in front of her and knew no one was behind her. She ran through the store yelping. On her way back since she knew I did the spiritual readings, she stopped for a minute to describe to me what had happened . She wondered out loud, "Who pinched me? Who poked me in the back room? Who touched me, my shoulder hurts." I said "Do you want me to try and figure it out?" "Yes." So I went to the back room, I was not really thrilled about it. I do not like scary stuff, but I went back and walked down the stairs and kind of got quiet. I came back and then I said "Someone was shouting "Alice, Alice, Alice you've got to pay attention to this, Alice, you've got to pay attention." The spirit appeared to me as wearing a uniform of some kind with a badge, with a very strong presence, loving. She was making it known that she would be there and that Alice needed to be paying attention to whatever it was. So I came back out and went to the girl and I told her that the spirit was shouting Alice and it turned out to be her mother's name and the woman spirit identified herself as Ruthy. The clerk acknowledged that Ruthy, her mother's very best friend, was deceased and the beach cop among other things and bus driver and always had a uniform on and presented in a very strict manner. This occurred around 1:30 pm. On the next day the clerk reported to me that yesterday was crazy enough but what happened was the mother (who was Alice) called her and told her at exactly 1:30p.m. the previous day, she was coming of the Doctor's office with the father, and he was told that he was having a serious heart problem that requires surgery. He did have the surgery, but a few weeks later he died.

Someone came to me for a reading because her father had passed. She was also surprised because a couple of weeks later she found a stone planted on her tire. I connected with the spirit of her father. I told her his name, I told her " Paul is around you and he says that as you were growing up, he didn't really share his love with you as much he should have and said " 'I really wasn't there for you the way I should've been but now I'm going to be your rock.'" Then he continued and said " 'By the way, thank you for the flag thing'." So I said this and she cried and said "Oh my goodness, he liked it?" She said they had a confederate flag; it was his treasured flag so when he died they put it up on the flagpole and she said she was so relieved to know that he liked that.

I was doing a reading for a woman who seemed very accomplished; her outside demeanor was polished and she seemed educated, composed and directed. She, however, wanted a reading to see what direction her life should take. I received information from a man named James and I told her I have James here and she looked at me and said, "That's my father who has been dead for many years." "Well he's pretty upset and a very intense feeling of apology and acknowledgment of something he was remiss about is coming through ." He said, " 'Sheila, I'm giving you something and I should've many years ago'." He showed me a present in a box, wrapped up like a Christmas present, and he opened it for me and inside on a piece of paper sort of were the words "self esteem" .She cried and cried and said he abused her, she never quite got over it and always felt like she needed to prove something .She was delighted. I said "When you go for your next interview, because I feel that you're switching jobs, know that your father does love you and you don't have to prove anything anymore. Go and present yourself and all of your accomplishments like you are talking to your father knowing that he approves already. It does not matter whether or not you get the job; it is a prop for you to explain to your father who you became after your "not so good" experiences with him and know and truly feel your father's respect." She was truly relieved and did not care anymore if she changed jobs. .She was quite amazed and thanked me for the surprising intensity and healing of the reading. She came to me a few weeks later to tell me that she got the job, even though she did not care at all at this time whether she got the elevated position.

I did a reading for Julie and we started walking and I immediately saw chocolate candy all around her and I said "I feel like your father is here and I feel like I'm getting the name David." She said "Yes that was his name." I said "I feel like he's offering you chocolate." She laughed and said she loved candy and he was always teasing her about how much candy she ate. He said if he were going to give her a birthday present, which was coming up, he would give her a bicycle helmet and she laughed and said that when she was 13 she fell and cut her head open. Then he started saying "Biblioteque" and that was in French and she said her father loved books and went to a French school and trained in a school in France." (All the names have been changed in these writings. As "Julie" was reading my manuscript, she relayed another interesting story. When she was a child, she and her siblings always rolled their bikes down the hill with ghost riders to whom they always gave fictitious names. She found it extremely powerful, that her ghost rider's name was Julie, the same name I " randomly" but I see not really, chose to substitute for her name in real life.).

I did another reading at somebody's house one day and I walked in the living room and there were multitudes of pictures on the walls, lots of family groupings and individual photos, high school graduate photos. I felt a pull to the photo with about 12 people in it and the spirits made me point to one young man in his late teens in the photo. The lady watched me and I hadn't even spoken yet and my finger went up and touched a young man and he told me that he was the one who died. I looked at her and asked "Is this who you asked me in your house to come into contact with?" And she said "Yes!" She started to cry and exclaimed, "My husband isn't going to believe this." Then I headed toward the far room where I was supposed to do the readings but was stopped by the boy's spirit. I said I really have to stay here by this picture and tell you things. He said he lived here when he died in this particular house. He said that in his closet she had to open the door and there were hooks in the closet- that there were two ties of his still hanging on them . She walked into the room speechless, that was his old bedroom, and she opened the closet and there were two ties on the hooks. Then he continued and said he had some sort of treasure box in there with metal things of some sort. She reached in the closet and opened the box and he had a collection of knives. These things can bring maybe one moment of peace to an individual.

I did a reading for a lady once, I told her "You attend parties at a big pool; there are lots of children, three generations. Your son, in spirit, goes there on these occasions and I'm getting the name Steve." She said "That's my sister's pool and my son's name is Steve." In that reading I also went to her house and we took a walk. I walked in a neighborhood that was not particularly familiar. I went around random blocks and we suddenly stopped at this traffic light and my feet would not move. She looked at me and said "That's where my son was killed; you unknowingly walked me to the exact spot where my son was killed." He was clearly showing us that he was okay.

In a reading I did an older woman, who was about 70 herself. She had lost her mother who was in her 90's very recently and was shocked no matter what ,that the best companion she ever had was now gone. I told her the spirit was here saying that she had tapioca pudding at the end. The woman cried and stared. " Yes you have my mother for the last thing that happened was that I gave her a spoonful of tapioca pudding and right then, she died." What better confirmation than that!

I was doing a reading for a woman and the spirits communicated to me that she had lost a son who was clearly too young to die. I saw a blue eyed young man with blond curly hair, about the age of 38. He told me he died suddenly of a heart attack. I heard the name Paul.

She acknowledged that this was all true. She had lost her son and his name was Paul, and that was the reason for her coming to me. He appeared to me in very colorful shorts and shirt. He was tanned and expressed that he was warm. It was clear that I was to emphasize how warm he was now. She cried and managed to tell me that he died of a heart attack while shoveling the snow and laid in the snow until someone found him sometime the next day.

I did a reading for this lady and the spirits came through and told me " 'Hi Jill!'" I told her that and she said that was in fact her real name. Her granddaughter Nancy was having some issues and she asked me to ask the spirits about it. They said "Well she has been doing some drugs and had been feeling alienated and what she really needed to do was pottery." They told me that it was important that when her soul came through to the human and did the pottery they worked together .This would maybe have her soul awaken and feel flowing again . The creativity while molding the pottery may become a conduit for the essence of the soul to manifest itself . It would be a connection for this disconnected person. Jill said "Oh she did pottery 8 years ago then she stopped it." I said "Well this is what she needs to do for her soul to feel alive again .Hopefully, there will be a change in Nancy."

So love and expecting to hear from the dead is what makes me tick right now. I hope all of you can get a reading. When you see there is another side maybe you will be amazed or happy or relieved and morph in a minute with a changed perspective.

PASS THE BATON

MY FATHER CAME TO ME A FEW DAYS AFTER HE DIED. HE CAME TO A PORCH I WAS SITTING ON AND SAID "HERE IS A PRESENT FOR YOU." I TOOK IT. IT WAS A CAREFULLY WRAPPED GIFT BOX AND I OPENED THE LID. INSIDE WAS A PAIR OF BINOCULARS. HE SAID "LOOK THROUGH THEM." I DID AND I SAW THERE WAS ATTACHED TO THE HOUSE A ROOM WITH DOUBLE GLASS DOORS. I LOOKED THROUGH THE CLEAR PANES AND SAW ELF LIKE OLD MEN BUSY WORKING. MY FATHER SAID "THEY ARE WRITING THE SCRIPTS FOR YOUR LIFE."

May the universe hug you. If it does not right now, maybe there will be magic in the next minute. If you think you are alone, you are not. No matter what you think, the other side watches and takes care of you and I love you. Good luck listening and watching for signs, synchronicity and the feeling that you are on a path led by other than humans. Even if you think there is no hope, there is. Life is always changing - always.

Face what you fear. Happiness is on the other side. I pass the baton to you. I share the love, knowledge and possibility of the other side with you. I share the wisdom of the sages on the other side. It seems as though dead people want to bear their wisdom. They say all across the board to love, forgive, believe. I pass the knowledge of hope that there is a better world and they watch us and can communicate with us through people like me and people as you are if you believe and become open. I pass on the baton of love and hope. Pass it on!

You do not know what the end is. This is the beginning of you creating the rest of your life. You have the power to edit some of your script.

HELLO

LIFE CONTINUES

MEDIUM
SUE BELLWETHER
PSYCHIC

REIKI
READINGS

508-965-1147

Breinigsville, PA USA
17 May 2010
238164BV00001B/1/P